Five for Sorrow, Ten for Joy

FIVE FOR SORROW
TEN FOR JOY

Meditations on the Rosary

J. NEVILLE WARD

Seabury Books
NEW YORK

First published in 1971 by Epworth Press.

A catalog record for this book is available from the Library of Congress.

ISBN 978-1-59628-012-0

Seabury Books
445 Fifth Avenue
New York, NY 10016

www.churchpublishing.org

An imprint of Church Publishing Incorporated

Printed in the United States of America

CONTENTS

Every meditation is a thought but every thought is not a meditation. We often have thoughts which have no aim or intention at all but are simple musing . . . and however attentive this kind of thought may be it cannot be called meditation. Sometimes we think attentively about something in order to understand its causes, effects, qualities; and this thinking is called study. But when we think about the things of God, not to learn, but to kindle our love, that is called meditating.

FRANCIS DE SALES,
Treatise on the Love of God

PREFACE

Several of my Roman Catholic friends have told me that many Catholics today are unable to pray with the rosary. There is nothing surprising in that—most forms of prayer and devotional exercise periodically die on you, some forever, and lose their power to express your religious hopes and longings. Negative associations from the past can make these practices uncongenial, as can over-familiarity (it can happen with the greatest music, so why not with a form of prayer?), or you simply may want to say something new to God.

We have to experience change and variety in the means we use for addressing God or else the life of faith becomes dull. People "go off" prayer for this reason; they need more varied spiritual fare in their lives. I realize that as a Methodist I have been lucky in coming to the rosary fresh, without memories or preconceptions, but like everyone else I want the stimulus of praying in new ways. An obvious way of doing this, in these days of increasing ecumenical encounter and exchange, is to attempt to turn to resources not used in our own tradition but widely employed elsewhere in the life of the church. There is a double advantage here: the stimulus of praying in a new way and the widening of our experience of the fellowship of the Spirit.

However, the desire for variety was not my only reason for turning to the rosary. There was also the fact of the Bible. It seems clear that the first-century Christians who put together the four gospels found they could not do justice to the mixture of divine and human in Jesus without saying some remarkable things about his mother. Their minds were continually drawn to her. Because they felt that to Jesus was given the name that is above every name, these early Christians sensed an extraordinary mystery about Mary. They knew as well as we do that the influence of a mother over a child is absolutely incalculable for good or ill. If Jesus was who they thought he was, then who was she?

The earliest Christian communities did not stay long in this realm of unknowing. Very soon they found themselves surrounding Mary's memory and her presence in the communion of saints with unique love and thankfulness. Nowadays the first-century birth and infancy narratives of Matthew and Luke are seen as a paean of praise to God and to Mary for Jesus. Since then there has poured through the life of the Christian church a flood of gratitude and love for her whose existence was the slender thread on which hangs so much of life's joy and meaning.

The western rosary considers fifteen forms of experience—five at its happiest, five at its most horrible, five at its most glorious—as seen in the life of Jesus and his mother. These are fifteen representations of reality. Nothing can happen to us that is not contained; all that is there can happen to us and in some sense is happening to us now. To pray the rosary is to try yet again to keep in touch with life in its fullness, to make sure we do not evade or miss anything.

The ring of beads is a means for counting prayers as we enter into the practice of prayer and meditation. There are five groups of ten beads, each group separated from the next by a larger bead. To this circlet of beads is added a short pendant consisting of a large bead, three small ones, another large bead, and a crucifix.

The rosary is used in various ways. A common way is to start with the crucifix at the end of the small pendant. On this bead the creed is said, then on the first large bead the Lord's Prayer, a Hail Mary on each of the three small beads, and the "Glory be to the Father" or the *Salve Regina* on the remaining large bead.

Where the pendant joins the round there is a large bead or a medallion on which is said the Lord's Prayer; then come ten small beads, each one for a Hail Mary; then a large bead for saying "Glory be to the Father." This concludes what is called "the first decade." The Lord's Prayer begins the next ten, and so on until the decade consisting of the Lord's Prayer, ten Hail Marys, and the *Gloria Patri* has been said five times, and the round is finished.

These memorized prayers are combined with a scheme of meditation on fifteen subjects, all drawn from the Bible with the exception of the last two. These subjects are called *mysteries* and are divided into three groups as follows:

The Joyful Mysteries
1. The Annunciation (St. Luke 1:26–38)
2. The Visitation (St. Luke 1:39–56)
3. The Nativity (St. Luke 2:1–20)
4. The Presentation (St. Luke 2:22–40)
5. The Finding in the Temple (St. Luke 2:41–52)

The Sorrowful Mysteries
1. The Agony in the Garden (St. Luke 22:39–54)
2. The Scourging (Isaiah 53:1–5; St. John 19:1)
3. The Crowning with Thorns (St. Matthew 27:27–31)
4. The Carrying of the Cross (St. Luke 23:26–32)
5. The Crucifixion (St. John 19:17–37)

The Glorious Mysteries
1. The Resurrection (St. John 20)
2. The Ascension (Acts 1:1–11)
3. The Coming of the Holy Spirit (Acts 2:1–13)

4. The Assumption of the Virgin Mary
5. The Queen of Heaven (Rev. 12)

While each decade of the rosary is said one of these themes or mysteries is held in the mind for meditation, so that each time the rosary is said the mind will have dwelt on five great Christian meanings. They are taken in turn according to the days of the week: on Monday and Thursday, the Joyful Mysteries; on Tuesday and Friday, the Sorrowful Mysteries; on Wednesday and Saturday, the Glorious Mysteries.

Such is this fifteen-point devotional practice for meditation in a setting of familiar prayers that has been found to be so helpful to innumerable people greatly varying in age and education and experience. No other scheme of prayer has been so widely used in the Christian west.

People unused to the rosary may hesitate over its most frequently repeated prayer:

Hail Mary, full of grace, the Lord is with thee.
Blessed art thou among women,
and blessed is the fruit of thy womb, Jesus.
Holy Mary, Mother of God, pray for us, sinners,
now and at the hour of our death.

When we say the Hail Mary we are looking at whatever aspect of Jesus' life (and Mary's, and ours) the mystery brings before our minds. The first part of this prayer, from St. Luke 1:28 and 42, is a way of bringing to mind our belief that the incarnation of the Son of God is the most wonderful thing that has ever happened in history and, therefore, of restoring the mind to the joy at the foundation of the Christian life. The second part of the prayer is a reminder that Christ has abolished our loneliness, that we pray (even if alone at home or in an empty church) within the fabulous community of faith, live within it, owe more than we know to it, and particularly rely on the prayers of others, the whole communion of saints, of which the Blessed Virgin Mary is the representative figure.

It seems hard to believe that one can meditate on a theme while mentally repeating certain prayers even though these are so thoroughly known that little effort is required. As one becomes familiar with the rosary the prayers gradually recede, to form a kind of "background music," and the mystery is before the mind as though one is looking at a religious picture or icon. The balance frequently changes, and the prayers occupy the foreground of the mind for a time, and this may lead to a form of simple attention to God which is more like contemplation. If one finds one's mind being led into a stillness and concentration of this kind it is good to let it happen. It is just a fact of Christian history that the saints put their faith in contemplation rather than meditation for creating a longing for God. And the longing for God, if it is not the ultimate treasure itself, is certainly the field in which it is hidden.

This movement of the mind between meditation and contemplation and petition and praise is a feature of this way of praying that gives it great flexibility and may well explain in part why it appeals to so many people so different in religious make-up. The images of the themes for meditation, the mysteries, tend to haunt the mind out of prayer, at any time and any place drifting in and out of one's preoccupied consciousness, sometimes only momentarily, sometimes staying to unfold new significances and relations to one's personal life, or simply bringing a breath from the world of God's action in Christ into the hurry and stress of the busy day.

Thinking about the mysteries outside prayer profoundly enriches the use of the prayer. It seems to me to be essential to the whole exercise. It is not possible to meditate discursively while actually saying the rosary. It is enough to have a single thought in connection with each mystery or simply to look at in love and faith. But the saying is infinitely deepened in value if we at other times think about these great themes, penetrating as far as we can into their meaning.

It seems to me impossible to use the rosary if we are not drawn to Mary, whose presence gives it its unique atmosphere. Although much has been written about Mary that I find quite uncongenial, some poetry and much art and music communicate marvelously the meanings God has given her to carry for the nurture of our spirits. Through all of this we hear the unmistakable call to love her and think about her, and about God's purpose for us all—to save us from evil and bring us through death into his presence. It is in part because I have found so few Marian prayers that touch my heart that I hold the rosary in my hands with such gladness—for its simplicity, its scriptural character, its unpretentious love, and its rightness for every occasion of joy or grief or perplexity that life in its time-driven course may bring.

Chapter 1

THE ANNUNCIATION

A ll people who pray have been given or have unconsciously absorbed some traditional idea of it—
Christian, Buddhist, Hindu, as the case may be. It may
well be that their understanding of their tradition is inadequate, they may indeed have got it all wrong, but that is
where they begin.

The Christian who has a rosary in his hands is within
a tradition. Certainly he misunderstands it, needs to learn
more of it, but he has to apply his mind to something
given. He does not have to seek the truth as though St.
Paul, St. Augustine, St. Thomas, and all the rest had
never lived. The person who starts from scratch and
attempts to reach the Christian view of the truth outside
the church has a long haul ahead of him. He will hardly
have time to live. He will be answering questions seven
days a week. In the Christian view the "answers" are
things by which one lives. The living is what matters.

Many people do not seem concerned that life may or
may not have any discernible meaning. They have their
own standards and aims, learned or picked up from a hun-

dred different sources, and they go about their lives without wishing to go any more deeply into such questions as the life of religion claims to answer, without feeling the need for the rational and emotional supports to living which religion claims to offer. They are in no way inferior to others more intellectually agitated. Many of them must walk with God in their active experience, in the acute sense of human misery and need that visits some of them with all the shock of an inspiration, in their awareness of the beauty and fascination of life. But a whole dimension of human life seems to be missing from their experience.

This dimension is one in which people experience an anxious need to understand. It is not simply that such people like the world of ideas. They belong to those for whom thoughts are not a game but a fight for survival.

Such people feel that to be able to go on it is necessary that what they do and suffer and enjoy should be justified in terms of a meaning that includes everything in its scope. They cannot settle for the imprisonment of the individual in his own privacy; they must relate somehow to all that they see to be going on, knowing at the same time that they must always register only a fraction of all that is going on. The possibility that there is no discernible meaning gives them an extremely unpleasant dizziness as though they stand precariously on some narrow rock ledge of the mind, below them the soundless gulf.

When someone says that life, or his life, has a meaning we conclude that he has adopted a certain view of life which brings order into his experience. It proposes values for his rational aspiration that excite his commitment. It enables him generally to act freely and interestedly and to regain his freedom and enthusiasm when adverse experience has submerged him in some compulsive reaction.

A political creed or some extensive moral aim can provide this kind of meaning as well as any of the great religious faiths. A genuine religious faith, however, involves the attempt to interpret all experience in its terms and consequently a greater investment of the self, as though a man would find himself in finding it and be lost in failing it. And it rates very highly certain moral and aesthetic experiences which shed an exceptional radiance over the mind or disturb it with unaccountably intense joy or sadness or desire to give. Such experiences always seem to have more in them than ever gets said.

Within the Christian tradition meaning is given to life in the form of a pattern of believing, hoping, loving that derives from the life and teaching of Jesus. The believer does not have to construct this meaning. It is there, among many other forms of believing, hoping, loving, waiting for his notice and interest as his awareness of the world develops. He chooses it because the man who first taught it has a unique magnetism and because it appeals to him as a reasonable interpretation of life.

Deep within this meaning is the conviction that life is to be interpreted as sign and lived as though human beings are continually being addressed or called to in one way or another. The process of nature, the flux of history, all that happens to each individual every twenty-four hours is "a mighty sum of things forever speaking." This way of thinking of experience in terms of speech-situation derives from the opening pages of the Bible. In Genesis 1:1–2:3 the whole evolutionary process is presented under the image of a God who "says" each element in it to bring it into being. And what he says is good. For the believer existence is not a neutral thing that one tolerates provisionally, waiting to see if one can like it or should hate it, but something about which to be glad immediately.

More particularly, what God "says" is one form or another of love. Every "word" that proceeds out of the mouth of God is to be seen as a form of his supreme, self-revealing, normative word, which is Jesus Christ. When St. John says "without him was not anything made that was made" (John 1:3), he means that nothing comes into being without what Jesus is; and since Jesus is, so

3

Christians believe, in himself a demonstration of God's love, St. John means that God can never act without loving. From the same world of belief, in a God who can only love, comes Jesus' mysterious saying that man is to live not just by bread but by every word that proceeds out of the mouth of God (Matthew 4:4). The idea that *life* is to be drawn from *every* word that proceeds from the mouth of God flings open a window in the mind onto an almost magical world in which everything is ultimately advantage, all is plus; even the dying that has to be done is part of a positive mercy of continual increase and fulfillment in the warmth of some eternal sun. To him who has the grace of this vision more will always be given. It will inevitably make the voices of life more numerous and mean more.

From these convictions comes the characteristically Christian view that every experience is a kind of annunciation, an announcement that God wishes us to receive something, do something, or endure something, and that, if we are willing to say "yes," our receiving, doing, enduring will be the occasion of the Eternal's revelation of himself in time again.

If "things proceed from the mouth of God like words," as de Caussade wrote in *Abandonment to Divine Providence*, so that life is indeed good and all that happens is to be referred directly or remotely to God's love, human beings can produce this "yes," this initially optimistic and trusting response to experience. They can do this because they take for granted a certain brightness in life in the light of which they will assume that it is innocent of any threat to their being until it is proved guilty. If each moment of a human life, whether it is one of beauty or boredom or panic, is an event in which there is a word from God, the right attitude to experience is a kind of listening and a readiness to say, "Be it unto me according to thy word."

No one can prove that this is the right way to interpret experience. The Christian simply says that this is how he understands it all. But it can be shown that it is not unreasonable to think this way. The Christian view is not inconsistent with any known fact. It is a way of understanding life in which human beings can think freely about it, live out their deepest moral and aesthetic concerns, and add to all that in the past has spoken in man's favor.

There are other readings of the complex pattern, some perhaps just as interesting. There need not be war between them but there certainly can be the interest of dialogue and mutual elucidation as well as experiment with new descriptions. It is fear that must at all costs convert.

The first mystery of the rosary concerns a God who speaks, who speaks through various messengers, who is therefore heard or not heard. He is never something or someone whose presence can be demonstrated.

He is one who speaks when man may not be listening and he is therefore somewhat at the mercy of man's interest and response.

He may say what man does not want to hear, what may challenge all his stabilizing codes and prudential arrangements. He is also one who may not speak at all, who can choose to be silent—for example, when man desperately wants to know what only God can tell him.

And he may say what man thinks hardly believable, that we are not alone, the long-desired friend is here, and life is heading for a fulfillment saturated with joy.

When the Virgin Mary hears this God she is made extremely lonely. She is isolated from the moral assessments of her time and from the one love of her life. She now knows something she hardly dares believe, dares not risk making known. She must go on as before, giving others no hint of its effect on her life if it is true, struggling with the thought that it might not be true, wondering whether that would be relief or some calamitous loss.

Many people have moments when they hear that which leaves them surmising that there may be something in religion, something for them. But this possibility of grace is often killed by repressing forces in society and within the self.

Over the years we have all unconsciously developed strategies of defense against new experience. The process begins deep in the forgotten world of our childhood, in rejections and hurts there, and becomes a cumulative though ill-defined sense that life is not a thrill but a threat. The threatened self stiffens, withdraws, erects defenses or moves aggressively against the world, and becomes formidably successful in keeping love and God at bay.

It seems that Jesus was dismayed at the havoc so caused. He argued the wisdom of remaining open to experience, ready to listen, waiting to respond, because God himself comes in everything that happens. He gave assurances that people who love life and let go their hold on all that defends them from the risks of love will not be lost. They will certainly gain in knowledge of the real world, because they will not unconsciously distort the facts. They will increasingly be able to live in and with all their feelings and memories, and to live in and with themselves as thinking beings. They will like being alive. In the Christian view, when life works out in the desire for more of it and the decreasing need for defensive denial or distortion of this or that ingredient of it, "the Lord is with thee."

Some people come to know this presence long before they give it a name. Some people never give it a personal name; some eventually give it the great religious name. This must be a marvelously happy way to come to God, experiencing the grace of things again and again and then in some moment of brightness and recognition seeing what the glory is, who he is.

But most people have to be told that the Lord is with them. To some it is an outrageous announcement because they have experienced so much of the injustice and contradiction of things. Actually, most people begin no more confidently than by living provisionally in the faith that he is there, that in the present situation the grace of life is waiting to take form through their accepting and doing God's will. The normal way in which Christian faith becomes real is first the announcement of the gospel, that you are greatly favored, that the Lord is with you and means to make the present substance of your life the bearer of his love and truth, and then your decision to see how it goes when life is lived in terms of that annunciation.

If God speaks, man must try to understand what he says. He must also understand what it means to listen.

At the basis of listening is a certain neutrality and stillness, inhibiting the evaluation of the situation in terms of preconceptions. There is the desire to understand, to see how anyone could think this way since many apparently do and not all are fools. A listener makes a deliberate attempt to enter the mental world of the speaker so that he reaches behind his inadequate vocabulary or inarticulateness to what he is trying to say; he does not lazily and unsympathetically stop at what his words can be made to mean. There is a certain mental agility that experiments to see if other words could be used and mean the same thing or nearly the same thing, along which route one might come closer to understanding.

And there must be courage, because there is the risk of being influenced by what you understand. If you listen to a well-informed communist who expresses his thought clearly so that you begin to "see things his way" you run the risk of seeing your own ideas and attitudes modify. Anyone who is not ready for this, who is unwilling to change, should never listen to anything beyond the jokes in the bar. To listen to what life says, in the many forms and voices in which it speaks, is the only way to avoid the world of private fantasy, the only way to be *present*. Unwillingness to listen is the decision in favor of one's imaginary picture of life; it is to play creator and make your own world and settle for your personal alternative to reality. Some of this we never stop doing. But it pays to reduce it, to give reality a turn; otherwise you could find yourself out of touch, not part of the living present, only part of the sweepings of time.

The Christian interpretation of life may seem unlikely at first, but the man who launched it was always talking about the real, the living, the new, the now. Movement and change were characteristic of him, especially change. He left the world an eternally youthful image of himself, not only because he died young and obviously had so much more to say and do. St. John hints that it would not be extravagant to call him the new Dionysus giving mankind the wine of life.

It is wise to acknowledge the difficulty of listening. The Bible has much to say about prophets doomed to have no response but people's deafness or their rage. Jesus seems to have been less furious, and less despairing in the face of the unlistening. He had a habit of concluding some comment on life with a saying about hearing and insight. He said it so often it is a kind of refrain, certainly a password to the mind of Jesus, "If you have ears to hear, then hear."

It never seems a particularly ingratiating remark but it is in fact a flash of light revealing his wide understanding of the human condition. When it is a matter of personal life that is shored up by some fantasy, clinging desperately to another time and another place, or hopelessly lost in emotional contradiction, the truth may be not bearable, in which case it is not the truth, the word of God for that person, or it may not have sufficient meaning for him just now to set him thinking in a constructive way. Truth has to have its moment.

It is always the moment for some truth, in the sense that God is present in every situation, wishing us to do or suffer or enjoy something, and ready to help this experience carry some fresh realization of himself and his purpose. And this is always blessing, always favor, because reality is on man's side and all that happens is for the production of mercy, pity, peace, and love within each life and throughout the world. To believe this is to face experience warm, with a hopeful, indeed expectant, attitude. It is going to be all right.

It is one of the principal exercises in any program of prayer to train the mind to bring these Christian considerations into focus at will, particularly recalling and trusting what we believe to be true about life as a whole when our world has contracted to some sharp bit that is cutting into us now. The training is a lifelong affair, very uneven, with many stops and fresh starts. There is always some part of us that shrinks from experience. It has been pointed out that this tension between willingness and unwillingness appears in innumerable paintings of the Annunciation.

> Mary is depicted as a young, childish innocent, carefully dressed and set down in a walled interior—nothing more than a schoolgirl at home in her room, often doing handwork or at her studies, who is suddenly confronted with the Angel. In her body redemption will be prepared. She is shocked, astonished. In her face horror and rejection mingle with acceptance. The motif occurs in men and women today. In that schoolgirl image of our dreams, in those too young emotions—too naive, too innocent, too self-centred—something redemptive can grow, which might in the end lead to our own redemption.... But in the beginning it is astonishment and shock, for somewhere we are all virgins, sensitive, shy, psychologically naive, unexplored in our emotional life, unwilling to be called into involvements... resistant to the major challenge, preferring where it is safe at home, familiar and protected, with books and bits of handwork.[1]

Chapter 2

THE VISITATION

The infancy stories in the first chapters of St. Luke's gospel are compilations of various materials, themselves related to religious needs in now untraceable situations, blended by imaginative conflation to form part of the Christian worship. They are expressions of the faith of the community who believed the risen Jesus to be the Son of God and saw all kinds of signs and anticipations of this triumph in their past, in the world of the Old Testament.

The poem that we know as the *Magnificat* is a fascinating and beautiful product of this process. It is mainly a collection of Old Testament quotations. This fact in itself stirs those who have a sense of history to retrace the long and mysterious transmission that finally set these words within the affection and faith of a thousand Christmases.

Time is present in every line of the poem. There is present mirth and present laughter, there is a backward look of gratitude to remotest beginnings in the past, and there is the thought of an endless praise from all human voices to come. This thankfulness and joy derive from seeing past and future in terms of God's continuous purpose to bring satisfaction to all mankind. The *Magnificat* is an outburst of joy about the beginning of the unique life in which we believe that purpose of God was made clear to us.

There are two strands of God's purpose, as the church understands it, woven into the joy of this poem. They concern, on the one hand, the built-in obsolescence, if not self-destructiveness, of all power and prestige as normally considered, the doom in things which brings to an end one "establishment" after another, and, on the other hand, the fact that those who live the undemanding and giving life experience the grace of things and find life lovable and accommodating, as though humility is infinitely creative and worth all the attention usually given to status and success in this world.

We miss the truth of this if we understand it as meaning that others are to be dislodged while we, the unnoticed, the not-very-successful, shall rise to eminence ultimately. The putting down and the exalting in the *Magnificat* refer to the spiritual dimension in which persons and churches and states discover the true value of things, and always at considerable cost.

The Christian today who uses the *Magnificat* in worship knows that the church itself is a notable example of the at-one-time-mighty now being put down. Enduring this—the pain of being brought low and struggling to understand why—and coming to insight into one's situation are part of the satisfaction and thankfulness to which God brings human life that is willing to be led by experience.

The meaning of the *Magnificat*, and indeed of the infancy stories as a whole, cannot be discovered without the consideration of their many Old Testament overtones. They represent Christian meditation on the truth as it is in Jesus in the light of Israel's past.

To pray by means of such scripture is to meditate on a distant generation's meditations on the Christ in relation to even earlier religious experience. The resulting sense of looking down the wrong end of a telescope into the dark backward and abysm of time brings right into one's praying the need to adjust to the mystery of the past.

The past is never entirely accessible to human investigation, even recent past, but always, even the remote past, a persisting influence. The life of the present is a river fed by innumerable streams whose sources no explorer will ever fully discover, however brave his journey into the interior of existence. To accept this is part of accepting the human condition, part of accepting the goodness of God. The whole truth, even of a small segment of life, will never be understood and told. Before this mystery, as T. S. Eliot wrote in *East Coker:*

> The only wisdom we can hope to acquire
> Is the wisdom of humility: humility is endless.

This humility has nothing to do with resignation and its modest aims and sad inertia. Humility is endless precisely because it is not resignation but faith, hope, and love, and there is no end to the relevance of this famous trio and their power to make sense of experience.

In the infinite relatedness of experience each of us has to connect as much as he can and make sense of as much as he can. Christians can do this with some optimism because they believe that Christ is central to the meaning of the whole.

Learning that Christ makes sense of life, and how, is the task of a believer's lifetime. Across the muddle of experience we build bridges of faith and love and make use of them. In this way life brightens with meanings, as long as we resist the temptation to ignore or disown what we think are the insignificant or intractable or discreditable items. E. M. Forster wrote in *Howards End* of the salvation latent in the soul of every man if he could stop living in fragments and see the universal relatedness of things. "Connect without bitterness until all men are brothers." For such an outcome the connecting must be indefatigable. We shall do it the more successfully the more we accept the continuity of life, that we exist only by virtue of the existence of others.

The setting of each individual's life comes home to him most vividly in the relationships of his family life. In our time these relationships have loosened so much that they appear to be disintegrating. Because the individual's attitude to authority in general is fed by the continuing influence of his early relationship with his parents, this loss of cohesion in the family is today associated with a radical criticism of all the traditional forms of authority. To many people this is part of the bewilderment and fear of our time, but the Christian believer is justified in seeing these facts in a different and much more hopeful light.

Concern about the life of the family should be diverted from the idea of authority to that of the kind of environment in which family happiness has its best chance. The young and growing human personality needs the regularities of a rational environment in which the logical ups and downs of pleasure and disappointment and affection teach one the nature of life and love. A child feels secure in such an environment though of course he will dislike it when it disappoints him. He feels insecure and mysteriously cheated if he is smothered in irrational love or has too much parental hope invested in him. The aggression that often develops in such a child is really his rage at not being able to love in return, at an emotional blockage he cannot understand and cannot remove.

There have been times when parental attitudes have been much influenced by the view that the child is basically in debt to his parents and owes them various duties—a view that is just as ridiculous and dangerous as its opposite, which is that the child is a creditor on whose innocent shoulders the parents in their selfishness have placed the burden of life. The Christian view is drawn from a vastly different world of thought. In that world of thought family life, whatever its difficulties, is always bathed in the light that is shed by the idea of the goodness of creation.

Science knows nothing of the goodness of creation because it merely describes and relates, it does not evaluate. Mere life, as it is transmitted through the act of procreation, is to the scientist observer neither good nor bad; the newborn child is simply potential being, a rudimentary center of pleasure and pain. But the Christian religion involves continual spiritual discrimination; and it "begins," on the first page of the Bible, with the determinative evaluation implied in the statement that God saw all that he had made and, behold, it was very good. In the Christian view, simply to be alive, with this two-sided possibility of joy and suffering, is good, which is why many Christians have been taught in their prayers to bless God for their creation as well as for their preservation and other blessings of this life. Therefore we must necessarily bless God for those two beings who, apart from anything else they subsequently did for us, gave us life.

But to be born is a package deal. Through our parents, helpless transmitters of heredity, there has passed into the structure of our being a psychosomatic deposit whose advantages and disadvantages we may partly recognize, need to recognize, but can never completely calculate. There is also a part of our inner life's substance which we owe to our parents themselves, as individuals in their separate time and place, as two lovers managing love both well and ill, and as father and mother. Some of all that they were in these respects no doubt passed over us leaving no trace, but some of it became a source of our richest personal life on which we shall draw to the day of our death, and some of it, against their intention, became areas of inhibition and aggression in our being with which we shall continually have to come to terms.

To bless God for our creation is to thank him for all this because to be alive involves all this and the Christian has decided for the inherent goodness of life. Particularly it means an initial thankfulness to the two beings who gave him life in these terms. His attitude to his parents is the outcome of his freely chosen interpretation of life rather than a matter of filial obligation derived from a code of commandments. We shall always do more good from a sense of the goodness of experience, from experience of the grace of things, than we ever shall from a sense of duty. This deep approval of the conditions of human life lies at the base of Christian thankfulness for the complex of joy and nostalgia and resentment that makes family life the searching experience it is.

Family happiness is always liable to founder on the hidden rocks and reefs of the unconscious life of its members. Christian acceptance of this involves the abandonment of all the extravagant expectations set up by the assumption that Christian family life ought to be a realm of frictionless loving. This in turn means that there will be less surprise and resentment and guilt when trouble comes and more chance of success in straightening things out. There is generally some straightening out to be done, human beings being what they are—creatures who do not as a rule do much harm except to those within range and most cruelly to those within closest range, brother, sister, parent, child, husband, wife. As Arthur Miller wrote in his play of that name, we encounter one another "not in some garden of wax fruit and painted trees, that lie of Eden, but after, after the Fall." But our lives are also the kind that are shaken periodically by beauty and other intensity of happiness, and again and again we know we are saved by love. This presence of love in family life is often unacknowledged, even unrecognized, because its nature is so much more akin to air we breathe than to thoughts we articulate.

> ... there's no vocabulary
> For love within a family, love that's lived in
> But not looked at, love within the light of which

All else is seen, the love within which
All other love finds speech.
This love is silent.[2]

In every family so touched by the Christian tradition that
at the back of everyone's mind is not only love's desirabil-
ity but its authority as the only ideal, there is inevitably
some repression of resentment, guilt, and aggression which
is accordingly projected onto other members of the family. Each member of course experiences the others differently, for which reason two brothers never have the same
father, but all will be driven at various times by the hidden
need to project their own guilt and fury onto the rest or
one of the rest. In many families the proverbial "black
sheep" serves as a scapegoat in this way, is indeed likely to
be so used quite apart from any inadequacies that may
justly be attributed to him or her. In the very first
Christian family the black sheep was Judas and, whatever
his own guilt, he certainly had laid on him part of the
iniquity of all that tragic group who knew they had failed
to love the Son of Man as he wanted to be loved and
should have been loved.

In this uncertain world of human emotion, in which
we often do not understand whom or why we are fighting,
the repudiation of the judgmental attitude by all is a
requirement of Christian spirituality. Grace is more relevant than law simply because it is more effective. It is
always worthwhile attempting to understand people, to
relate their behavior to its possible causes, to note what
one imagines to be their personal resources of courage,
humor, flexibility (or their lack of these), and to leave the
assessment of their responsibility for their failures to the
end of time when, it is believed, someone will appear with
competence for this dangerous exercise.

To pray for one's family, as for others whom one meets
daily or frequently, is part of the Christian way of living,
which is to say that it is part of what Christians mean by

loving. Our reactions to people are always "remotely pre-pared" (to use an idea from traditional Christian prayer) in the sense that how we think about them when they are not present determines how we treat them when they are. What we desire for them in our solitary reflections tends to be partially, if not wholly, realized in our subsequent dealings with them. These desires are sometimes for their harm, as when through being hurt by them or disappoint-ed in them we cannot forgive them and so cannot stop the inner flow of aggressive brooding and complaint. Sometimes we do this unintentionally, unaware that we are on the wrong side of their life, when we want what we mistakenly think is their good.

There are many reasons why we may easily misconstrue God's will for people we love. Our insight into their per-sonalities, what they most secretly fear and want, may not be very penetrating; or we may not understand any human life sufficiently, the strain of its inner conflicts, its lonely waiting for some overdue grace; or we are unaware of our need to see the loved person develop according to some role we have prescribed for him or her.

These unrecognized personal needs and inadequacies take from our loving much of its genuineness. It is not pos-sible to love at all unless the loved person can be seen in some other light than that of our personal needs and long-ings. Prayer counteracts the twist given to our loving by the demands of the ego. To pray for someone in the Christian way means to see him in a new light that is both more objective and kinder than that shed by our needs and demands. Recollected in tranquility, and in Christ, the individual for whom we pray is detached from the experience or experiences which have invested his image with so much emotion and he becomes what he truly is—a child of God making his unique way to the source of his being and the place of his natural joy. He is doing this very much alone, in the essential solitariness that life is for everyone, and, like everyone else, he will succeed only as his capacity to give and receive love is encouraged to unfold. To pray that this may happen, that God's kingdom may come to him and God's will be done by him (and there is nothing so much worth praying for) is irrational unless we are ready to give free course to whatever of this grace is meant to enter his life through ours. This makes us less sure that we know what is good for him, more sure that we want God's best for him, and it brings us all together in our common need of the merciful help of God.

St. Luke's picture of the Virgin Mary's visit to her cousin Elizabeth and the conversation of these two happy expectant mothers in the hillside home may suggest to some people cozy thoughts of woman's realm, but that would be unfortunate. The need today is to challenge this traditional separation of male and female experience. In the general ferment of ideas about men and women in relationship there can be discerned new possibilities of richer personal relations than humanity has ever known. These will not be realized unless men and women learn to be truly present to one another as well as physically together, sharing their deepest and most sensitive experience of life and, if they are Christians, learning to speak about the mystery of the Christ each carries within.

The word "love" has been treated so carelessly and taken into so many doubtful places that it has now an embarrassing look and needs to be put through some cleaning and tidying process of redefinition. If the word is used for the relationship of two human beings in marriage it must be understood as at least that happiness that derives from a man and a woman rejoicing in the truth of each other's being.

Such love involves seeing something of the other's true self, the self God wishes him or her to be, and letting that self be, indeed helping it to be. It needs courage to let one another be. When two people marry who need but do not know one another it is a question whether they can bear the emergence of each other's true being, and they may be driven to all kinds of evasion and injury to prevent the growth of the other's true self.

The fulfillment of marriage is that joy in which each lover's true being is flowering because its growth is being welcomed and unconsciously encouraged by the other in the infinite series of daily decisions which is their life together.

Chapter 3

THE NATIVITY

Children are not given much room in the sacred liter-ature of the great religions. Certainly the world of the Old Testament takes little notice of them. They seem far less important there than animals, and they represent, along with sheep and oxen and changes of raiment, how much their parents are worth. The mind of Jesus worked differently. What children are in themselves seemed to intrigue him. The world they share with their friends, so fragile and yet so mysteriously protected from adult inva-sion, carried significances infinitely worth exploring by people at every stage of life.

Why he should have seen so much in the realm of childhood it is impossible to say. Some people have a childhood so beautiful that it will not let their minds go, or so unsatisfactory that it breeds a hopeless longing for this crucial bit of the human joy they have been denied. Jesus never had the adventure and fulfillment of marriage and children, but the fact that he drew so much important imagery for the life of faith from the world of childhood suggests that the memory of his earliest days, graced with the beauty and love of one particular face, was part of the deep joy within his being.

There are people who cannot see his joy. Albert Camus saw a certain darkness in Jesus, "that sadness that can be felt in his every act." He wondered if this was to be traced to his coming to know of the tragedy his birth is said to have set in motion, the murder of so many innocent children. Certainly Jesus was born in the sin and grief of others, as everyone is born; yet his birth is for all Christians the start of their happiness. The Christian policy is to keep continually in view this curious ambiguity of life. We are not born in sin in the sense that some ineradicable evil attaches to the sexual function but in the sense that we are born in a world of sin and grief, and goodness and joy, and we soon become involved in all this as givers and receivers. In every birth the enterprise of life is tried again, so once again there is the chance of happiness, there is hope, and, because the world is what it is, there is anxiety and the certainty of failure unless grace descends.

During the last twenty years the popular version of Christianity among the *intelligentsia* has been humanist and nonmetaphysical. Silent or patronizing on the major questions that have haunted religious man, it has in effect been the bland moralism of the liberal theology again, though somewhat more strident. It is interesting that during all this time a much grimmer voice has been heard in the theater, in the drama of disintegration, cruelty, and the "absurd." We overdo God's reputation for moving in a mysterious way. He seems to get his word uttered. And if the church refuses to state the possibility of hell he announces it elsewhere, perhaps has to overstate it a little, in the arts. In many serious plays and films of our time is to be heard a voice that is truly radical in the sense that it goes to the root of what is the matter with us all, even if it cannot yet give us much to hope for or much to trust. It is because the truth as it is in Jesus faces heaven and hell with a full consideration and turns our anxiety into faith and hope and love that the church is always giving thanks for him.

"This is a true saying, and worthy of all men to be received, that Christ Jesus came into the world to save sinners." Many people wonder whether this saying is worth such universal reception. They argue that today if anyone finds the Christian faith speaking to his condition it is not because it offers forgiveness. It is not guilt that disturbs our generation but the sense of meaninglessness, the suspicion that death finally adds up all the columns and makes them come to precisely nothing, and the helplessness of the individual to make any impression on the great unseen forces that control the political and international life of the world. If Christ can save from those versions of the human malaise it would be strange if Christians frowned on people settling for so much. The fact is that the sense of sin now comes much later in the experience of grace than it used to do.

When someone begins the life of faith it is some form of freedom he now wants first, release from the half-discerned bonds that hold back his power to love and enjoy, from the fear of certain aspects of his experience that reveal his incompetence, from the inertia that quickly sets in should he conclude that nothing is worth his ultimate concern.

As he "learns Christ," however, he discovers that more of himself is going to be involved in the process, that his being freed reveals to him his aggressions and exaggerated expectations and the trouble they are to him. It is part of the hopefulness of the Christian view of life that our wraths and demands can be regarded as sins, that is to say, as emanating from that realm of our being in which we are at any rate in part free. They are not entirely located in the necessity of existence which we can only accept, resignedly or resentfully or despairingly. They are sins, actions that can be confessed as personally chosen and therefore forgivable.

The view that man is a sinner is the only truly hopeful view of him. It is a religious view, of course, and implies the Christian way of thinking about God without which it makes no sense at all. In the Christian faith God is by definition the one who is on man's side, has acted decisively to declare this, and means to win him by countless, infinitely varied persuasions to move out of his loneliness into the realm of perfect love.

There is certainly no hope for man if the wrongness in human lives is the result of social and hereditary forces beyond human control or is to be explained in terms of psychological sickness. A person can start hoping the moment he stops regarding himself as a victim and sees himself in Christian faith as a sinner. We are, of course, all to some extent victims, and how much we can never know, and this is why in learning Christ the believer learns to be very nervous about the risky game of blaming people for their disasters and eventually abandons it. However, in order to live life with dignity and self-respect and hope each one of us must believe in that blessed margin of his experience in which he can say "through my fault, my own fault, my own most grievous fault." He will need help in tracing the boundaries of this area of personal life and may often get it wrong, but the belief that human responsibility is a reality is part of the gospel.

But this sense of sin does not usually come at the beginning of the life of faith. Normally people now come to interest in the Christian understanding of life because it appears to them to be reasonable and likely to make sense of their experience, or through some sense that the aims and assumptions of their current living are unsatisfactory and such knowledge of Christianity as they have leads them to think that things may go better if they learn the Christian way.

For this beginning to have any chance to develop into faith it needs to be looked after, as a child has to be watched, fed, loved by his mother. Leave it alone and it will die. There is much more to be gained from seeing the spiritual life in this human way, in terms of birth and growth and need and nourishment, than in terms of the exceptional, of prophetic vision or charismatic grace or baptism of the Spirit. This does not mean that such rarefied forms of the spiritual life are not valid, but simply that they are exceptional.

Most of us are not ecstatics, martyrs, mystics, prophets, but we tend to hanker after sensation in religion. It may be just that we want to be rather distinguished in the life of faith or that we assume that the pedestrian is never the divine. The fact is that religion is quite dull most of the time, as E. M. Forster observed life is, and its chores have the infuriatingly necessary look of chores. Faith grows only through a continuing program of worship, prayer, reading, thinking, observant exploration of the world of loving, learning how to be silent.

This program is not in itself exciting, though quite often this or that part of it may leave in the mind a certain contentment, the conviction that it is right to do this. It pays off slowly, cumulatively, and some of its most important results are apparent only to others, the Christian himself often being unsure how things are going. What goes to make a Christian is in principle no more interesting than what goes into the training program of a football team or the exercises of a *corps de ballet*. The public worship of the church, for example, cannot normally grip anyone not interested in faith. It will naturally give the impression of an unfamiliar dimension of experience; if it also seems real and serious and suggests that it concerns the mystery in which all human life is lived, it will have done all that it can do and accordingly it must rarely do as much as this. There is no reason why the best possible worship should appeal to a mind undisturbed by any longing. Christians have always believed that their worship has a subsidiary function of witness and sign to the unbelieving world, and even that it is offered in some deeply discerning and affectionate sense on behalf of that world; but its principal purpose is to help the worshippers in their common journey

to God and the true life, and its effectiveness is not meas-
ured by their reaction to a single or several services but by
their prolonged experience of the common life of the
church of which worship is an important part but only a
part. The full program of this common life is meant to give
breadth and depth to the desire for God and to liberate
the love inside us that without God can only express a
fraction of itself.

Jesus spoke of all this longing for God and life and lib-
eration as involving a certain turning and becoming like a
child (Matthew 18:3). This cannot mean some rediscov-
ery of lost innocence. It is a sentimental delusion to imagine childhood as a world of innocence. Earliest infancy is
a pre-moral world in which innocence and guilt have no
meaning at all. Once a human being crosses the invisible
boundary which separates that kind of life from that in
which there is knowledge of good and evil, he seems never
to be innocent, but, in the Christian view, he can be forgiven; and this, being God's will for us in time, must be
better than innocence.

Nor is there any premium to be set on the child's exclu-
sion from the adult awareness of the complicatedness of
life, or on his having his youth, indeed practically all his
time, in front of him, compared with adults who have lost
their youth and do not know what proportion of their
dwindling hour remains. It is God's will that we shall
know good and evil, that we shall be young and grow out
of our youth as a youth grows out of his clothes. To want
any kind of reversal of this and to get back somewhere
behind the defeats, where all that has happened to us is
still ahead, must be regarded as one form of the sin against
the Holy Spirit, the Lord and Giver of life.

To turn and become a little child must mean not to
turn back but to turn into a different road, an alternative
way of dealing with life. For Jesus, this alternative attitude
to the human condition had certain features that suggested the world of childhood.

He saw the child as not sharing adult competitiveness and prestige hunger. It is not that children are humble—there is something seriously wrong with them if they are—but that a child in a satisfactory home feels secure and so does not develop the excessive, because defensive, need for power and safety in a threatening world that characterizes the strategies of withdrawal and aggression which so many of us adopt in order to get by.

Turning and becoming a child must therefore mean at least jettisoning this need for position, for "standing," and so being willing to be knocked down. It means being exposed and vulnerable. Jesus worked out this idea more fully in his teaching about the unproductiveness of anxiety, about living as carefree as the birds who "neither sow nor reap nor gather into barns, yet your heavenly Father feeds them" (Matthew 6:26). We do not know of anyone who looked on life with eyes as shrewd and penetrating as his, and it did not escape his notice that the life of the birds is by no means so idyllic, that in fact our heavenly Father does not feed them all. Some fall to the pounce of the cat, the swoop of the hawk; some starve to death in winter frost. If the birds are carefree it is not because of anything they know but precisely because, lacking the faculties of memory, anticipation, and reason, they cannot be anxious. They are simply exposed.

> Ultimately it is quite unimportant whether a man dies of hunger, whether he is well or ill. God has not undertaken to see that his disciples fare well in this.... Fear calls forth the desire for security, but faith demands that the heart should abandon itself to the unknown God.[3]

If we, with all our apparatus of rational mind, are to live carefree lives it can only be through realizing that the point of comparison between our life and that of the birds is not their animal immersion in the instant but their exposure to all the weather there is, and then choosing to live the life of faith. This is what it means to become like a child. It means to "look before and after" and still to trust life, because its conditions are determined by a loving God, and to dwell on this continually until we find we can drop our defenses and resentments.

The opposite of becoming like a child is to long nostalgically for one's childhood. Normal children look forward, want to grow up, rarely even play at being children. To be like a child would mean always looking forward to life, with as keen an interest at sixty as we did when we were six. To want to be six, or sixteen, again is to be on bad terms with the human condition.

Life's movement is our salvation. There is no way back to the self we were before the disappointments and resentments persuaded us to adopt so many mistaken attitudes. We can only go forward, but we can choose another route. We can expect the grace in things rather than their devilry.

And this is the famous repentance, or change of outlook, that opens the cheering recommendations of the message of Jesus. He says, in effect, that along this new route life looks and is so different that it is as if the self is being remade, reborn, is starting again. Like a child unburdened with the adult load of memories that produce so many frightened or obstinate prejudgments of experience, the man of faith sees all things made new, indeed truly sees them for the first time.

It is part of the Christian tradition that Christ was born in the night. The life-giving truth often comes to human beings in some kind of mental night as they endure and try to understand it.

The night is the dark side of life in which the familiar shape of our world dissolves and we lose some of our usual confidence, can indeed lose our way. In this unnerving darkness is set the gift of sleep, a gift because we have to receive it without any exertion, without any taking, we have only to let it come. The night is God's daily reminder that we are creatures with many limitations who can stand

even sanity only so long and must after sixteen or seven-
teen hours of it give up.

Since half of our life is lived in the dark it is not surprising that we draw on the vocabulary of night to express
some of our daytime experience. We are "in the dark"
when we are at the mercy of the unknown in ourselves or
our future or are suffering without any sign that anyone
cares or understands. This is to see only one of the many
faces of night.

The night is not only a realm of helplessness and fear.
It is the dispenser of healing, restoration, and insight as
well. It is this positive and congenial aspect of night that
is present in the implications which Christians draw from
the tradition that the definitive coming of the truth and
love of God was in the night. All our human darknesses
contain not only the formidable but, somewhere, hidden
and needing some search and identification maybe yet
nevertheless *there*, that which is *for* us, on our side.

When we cannot strike any spark of happiness out of
life and feel threatened with disintegration we may therefore ask whether or not some part of our personal truth is
coming to birth in that night. Perhaps we are being told
by the love that is as much at work in our unconscious as
in our conscious life that our current way of coping with
reality is too restricted or unrealistic or unnecessarily
wasteful. It may never have been truly us but some style
forced on us by our social or religious environment, or it
may have been chosen by us but mistakenly, through fear,
or it may be just no longer of use to the person into whom
we are now changing. Anyway, the darkness of this challenge is not meaningless. It is the divine presence making
clear our need of that broadening and relaxing of the self
to which Christ points the way.

He is for believers the marvelous realist, a messenger
from the world of reality from which human beings are so
often alienated. His message of the kingdom-at-hand is of
a happiness just round the corner of everyone's life

because its acquisition depends only on a change of attitude and stance in virtue of which we discover that what
we thought was life's intractability is really life's gracious-
ness, its endless creativeness. The gospel is an invitation
to learn this way of looking at experience, from him, at
the price of trust in his version of the way things are.

There is also a dark side of the self to be included in
this broadening and relaxing, the "shady character" within who trips us up when our aims are too mercilessly high
or when we struggle to keep too strict a control on our
lives. Everyone has his dark side as naturally as every day
has its night. In primitive superstition the only one without a shadow is the devil. We are not truly human, certainly not part of the kingdom of light, if we try to disown
or reject our inner darkness. The negative aspects of our
make-up disconcertingly reveal our imperfections, but
when understood and accepted they become our deeper
understanding of what it is to be human, the usable energy of a self functioning now more wholly.

Christian believers have made much use of the image
of night for the life of faith generally considered. As they
have tried to live it, it has often seemed more like the
night than the day in that most of the time what we
should do and think for God and about God is not given
us in a luminous certainty and his presence in our lives is
not located in any recognizable sensation. We have to
learn to live with mystery, doubt, and uncertainty but at
the same time, as we share the prayer and faith of the
church in depth, we learn to interpret life increasingly as
God's presence, so that our occasions of thankfulness
steadily gather and find their summary expression in the
one great thankfulness for Christ which is at the center of
the world-wide Christian joy.

One of the most enduring and helpful statements of
this peculiar quality of our relationship with God was
given by an unknown writer in the fourteenth century
under the title *The Cloud of Unknowing*. The writer argues

that at whatever stage we are in the Christian life God is calling us to a further stage. He assumes the place of prayer as the chief nourisher of faith and recommends that we aim at cultivating an attitude that is simply one of longing desire for God and continuing love of him. It is by this blind wanting and trust that communion with God comes, not by thought, not by feeling; indeed the mind in prayer is a kind of blank, functioning in a "cloud" of unknowing or ignorance. This state of not being aware of God's presence, but keenly wanting his action in one's life so that one can know and do his will, and trusting that in one form or another that action is going on—this is the prevailing atmosphere of the life of faith. There gradually develops a disregard of incidental feelings and a deepening confidence that all the time, whatever happens, we are in God's presence and can trust that the next step will become clear and we shall be offered sufficient grace to take it.

The answer to all our prayers, the response to all our spiritual effort, is not some special private disclosure from God for us alone, but the increasing realization that Christian faith, hope, and love form the most relevant and desirable way to live, whatever our circumstances. Every so often there are moments of joy and intense conviction as life takes on a sudden radiance. But the peace that passes understanding is the deep undertone of meaning and trust by which we know that everything happens within the love of God.

Chapter 4

THE PRESENTATION

Every human being is born at a place and time in which the word "God" is already there, a cluster of meanings he does not invent. He may reject them consciously or they may become just part of the destroyed magic of child-hood or he may be deeply involved in his own appropria-tion of them, but they are always in the first place given, part of the mental landscape of the world into which he is born.

Jesus was born into a tradition in which the word "God" was particularly associated with a never-to-be-for-gotten communal deliverance in the past and with many religious customs of even earlier origin. This complex past was powerfully present in the procedures that had to be observed at his birth by his parents, as by all parents of a firstborn son.

On the eighth day after his birth the child was circum-cised and also usually given his name. When he was a month old his parents had to make a money payment to the religious authorities, a custom which expressed the idea that the child really belonged to God as soon as born and had to be in a sense bought back by his parents, though he was never felt to be wholly theirs. When he was six weeks old his mother went to the temple for a "churching" ceremony which included a further offering. After this she could feel at ease in her social and religious world having done all that institutional religion prescribed.

It is part of the Christian view of life that a child belongs to God and not to his parents. Christian spirituality has always recommended a certain detachment from things, people, and events because it is a religion of freedom. However, to relax one's dependence on things and people and one's desire to control them requires a fundamental sense of security. We often do not feel safe enough to do this, but it is clear that the sense of security grows as we try to practice this detachment and makes us able to do more of it.

It is a help to question the whole concept of possessing. The Christian view is that we *own* nothing because the earth is the Lord's and the fullness thereof, though Jesus once considered the idea that all belonged to the devil (Luke 4:5–7). Whatever is now ours by good fortune or personal ability and work may easily be taken from us by misfortune or personal failure and is certainly put in its place by the thought of death. It is best seen as an allowance for uses and enjoyments that will serve our own and our neighbors' freedom and happiness. As Forster writes, "Injustice and greed would be the real things if we lived forever. As it is we must hold to other things because death is coming. I love death—not morbidly, but because He explains. He shows me the emptiness of money. Death and Money are the eternal foes. Not Death and Life." The "other things" we must hold to because of this sharp sense of mortality have been variously described by different religions and moralities. A classical Christian definition is the one used by St. Ignatius at the beginning of his *Spiritual Exercises*.

Man is created to praise, reverence and serve God our Lord, and by this means to save his soul. All other things on the face of the earth are created for man to help him fulfill the end for which he is created. From this it follows that man is to use these things to the extent that they will help him to attain his end. Likewise he must rid himself of them in so far as they prevent him from attaining it. Therefore we must make ourselves indifferent to all created things, in so far as it is left to the choice of our free will and is not forbidden. Acting accordingly, for our part, we should not prefer health to sickness, riches to poverty, honour to dishonour, a long life to a short one, and so in all things we should desire and choose only those things which will best help us attain the end for which we are created.

Freedom and happiness, in the Christian view, do not consist in the acquisition of things, but things are there for the making of human happiness. This principle implies a respect for things, an understanding and love of the material world without which that world cannot be set at the service of human joy. The ignorant and shortsighted manipulation of the material world serves death rather than life.

In the parental situation there is a sense in which nothing is so much ours as our children. Because they are products of our being most truly ourselves in love, and made from our bodies, they become extensions of our egos. They arouse in us appropriate emotions of protection and pride and they confuse us in the deepest realm of the self so that we are uncertain where the boundaries of our identity and theirs fall.

Just as Jesus' parents had to go through a ceremony which expressed the idea that their child was in fact not theirs but God's, so most Christian baptism services express the same conviction, puncturing the bubble of parental pride on the day when in the family gathering it is most ebullient.

Those who have seen the ship of faith go down must inevitably try to crowd as much of life as possible on the fragile raft of personal relationships. But it will not carry all we want it to save. It will not survive the last huge wave of death. The Christian believer is committed to a less anxious, because more detached, view of people and things.

We do not know whether the parents of Jesus found these traditions of institutional religion helpful or irritating. They may not have understood them sufficiently to question them. However, they may have found a new intelligibility in these particular ceremonies because in them religion at last concerned them personally and the new joy and depth that had come into their life.

Today institutional religion is low in the estimate of both believers and unbelievers. The old argument that religion is a strictly personal matter died many years ago but it refuses to lie down and still makes converts among the *intelligentsia*. There is of course much private seeking of a religious kind, for a meaning to life, for a set of values sufficiently clear to give existence some shape, and no one can desire any other result than that such seekers may find what they want. The Christian religion, however, is inseparable from its community, its tradition as to what is rightly to be said about God and man and what man can expect from life, its organized presence in the world, and its continuing debate with it. It is not possible to find out what Christians mean by the word "God" except in their company. Jesus came to know God by a similar route.

> For Jesus to put himself in the way of being anything to
> do with the Kingdom of God, he must have come to
> know God, humanly speaking, through the people of
> God, who already knew God, who already had experi-

ence which gave content and form and impact to knowledge of God.[4]

The same is true today for entry into Christian experience
with the people of God. Institutional religion will always
exasperate us because it is carried in the words and deeds
of inadequate and sinful human beings. Nevertheless,
there is no other way of knowing that Christ is risen and
really present in this our life than in the only group that
believes this and exists to hold this belief before the world.
The church is certainly composed of inadequate and sinful people (is there any other kind?) but this regrettable
characteristic makes it a particularly suitable sphere for
practicing as well as learning Christianity.

People who attempt to learn Christianity while rejecting institutional religion develop impoverishments and
distortions in their spiritual life which are clearly traceable
to this rejection. Baron von Hügel put first among these a
certain incompleteness in one's humility when it is exer-
cised before God alone, without recognition of my need of
other human beings, particularly those who are wiser and
better than I, and without recognition of my need of a
training and discipline framed by others and by the presence of others. Two other familiar dangers dog the foot-
steps of those who attempt to go it alone: the tendency to
settle for a moralistic, "Golden Rule" type of inchoate religion, and the likelihood of intellectual superiority, particularly among the educated.

Without organization, without the church, the
Christian faith must necessarily be left to the private
interest of individuals who may easily grow bored with
looking for God and may never care whether others find
him or not. Its prospects then would not interest any
insurance company. This is not to say that there is anything sacrosanct about any of the administrative or intellectual forms of the church which is by definition always

under the mercy and judgment of God, always in part usable, always needing reform.

The account of Jesus' parents presenting their child in the temple provides an image of the tension between form and vitality in religion. A formal routine of great antiquity is being observed, but it brings the Word of God, the true Light, into the sanctum of religion. This Light is later going to question the official exponents of religion, drive out those who merely use and so corrupt religion, and argue the coming destruction of the whole system. This is a pattern of much that was to come. The history of the church does show that the divine creativeness and destruction are carried right into the being of the church through its institutional life, unsatisfactory though this must be, not through the departure of angry people who are furious with it. All they do is leave a hole in it.

St. Luke's account of the "churching" of Mary includes a picture of an old man who has lived a long, waiting life, struggling to make sense of existence, believing in some coming moment of coherence. This moment was understood by his race as certain, as in some sense promised (it had not seemed to them possible that the truth could be sad), but in his case it had seemed tantalizingly delayed.

The passage was evidently written out of much Christian experience of the moment of understanding when the light dawns, one sees in Jesus the key to the meaning of life and hears an irresistible call to commit oneself to him and what he stands for, so that already one's values begin to change. The writer presents this central Christian experience through an old man of the old religion, the infant Jesus in his arms, saying in a fantastic happiness that now he can die because his brain has at last been given the truth that makes sense of life. He can die happy because making sense of life necessarily involves making sense of death. So in some churches at Candlemas there is a procession with candles to the singing of *Nunc dimittis*, which is a way of saying that everyone can depart in peace now that Jesus has poured around death the bright light of his Father's house.

The old man blesses the parents of Jesus as he stands with the wonder-child in his arms, a phoenix symbol of new life burning up from the dying fire of old Israel. A blessing is a declaration that the goodness of God is with the person blessed, that what God has to offer—himself, the ultimate joy and fulfillment of life—is already initially with that person and is to some degree more with him because of this blessing, because it is announced by someone (a father, an old man, a bishop, a priest) who has some recognized authority or knowledge of God or association with God that gives effective power to his blessing.

The words that accompany the blessing reveal its hidden depths as Simeon says to Mary, "This child is destined to be a sign which men reject; and you too shall be pierced to the heart. Many in Israel will stand or fall because of him, and thus the secret thoughts of many will be laid bare." Argument and hostility are going to gather around Jesus' unlucky head. This disturbance will be no surface affair, it will concern the truth itself and what each one of us is as a naked self, not the impersonations in which we hide. There may be some who will not be in the slightest affected by what happens around Jesus and to him, but not his mother. It will go through her like a sword. Yet in the end it will mean that many, perhaps all, will know the fulfillment of humanity's deepest desire, which is for God and his joy.

This ambiguous forecast of suffering and joy is the blessing of God as the New Testament understands blessing. To be blessed means to be included in the purpose of God and that purpose is worked out through human freedom, through people being wrong and right and losing and winning and learning what we must and what we need not accept. A painless life, in time, would be a curse, not a blessing; it would be a life outside the movement of all that matters.

"And you too shall be pierced to the heart." What was to pierce Mary's heart has been traditionally called a sword; and for the mind molded by Christian praying, reading, thinking, the sword is a symbol of dramatic density. The Word of God whose voice penetrates to the innermost self is said to be sharper than a double-edged sword (Hebrews 4:12). Truth must inevitably be sharp to the mind that has not cared about truth, imagining there is an easier route through life but now hopefully, nervously proposing to try reality. Christ is the supreme word of God, the one who says as much as God can say to man through man about how it is and could be with us. He questions perhaps more than we are willing to have questioned, laying bare without indulgence but always healing and restoring, in "the sharp compassion of the healer's art" setting people on the road to health and wholeness.

On this road we meet death of one sort and another, many times, before the one death from which all our images of finality and destruction derive. The self that clings passionately to some other place and some other time will die as the God of truth, of here and now, enters into it, as will the self that has chosen to live in other ways that are not true to it or not true to life.

There is a kind of death in losing what is in itself good but has to be jettisoned simply because you do not see how it can be included in the will of God for you just now. The cup of consciousness can be full to the brim but it can never contain all possible good. One of the crucial moments of human experience is the realization (by some odd mercy withheld from the young) that there is not enough earthly time for all that one could do and enjoy. So everyone selects, by various principles (though some let the spirit of the age do the selecting), and pays the price of his choices and exclusions. Some of this price, in the Christian view, can bear the name of suffering.

By "suffering" Christianity has always meant primarily not the end of beautiful situations, the loss of things and the death of persons we love, but the pain that comes through having chosen to act and react according to the Christian interpretation of life, the redirection and training of the self involved in this, and our experience of the world's resistance because we are living by this unpopular scheme.

The suffering that is part of the human condition, the anxiety, poverty, disaster, and death, is what human beings of perception realize has to be taken for granted, as part of the work God has cut out for us to do: it is not the sword, it is just the unequally distributed dark side of human life.

And the sword that went through Mary was all the pain that came from seeking to be at God's disposal in her time and place as she played her role in the Christian drama, all that was involved in being what she could be to him and letting him be what he could be to her.

> The sword of the word of God will make plain the thoughts of her heart, will test her faithfulness and prove her faith, and it is through much suffering experienced in her flesh and in her soul that she will know the victory of faith and the spiritual resurrection of which Simeon speaks. In that, as mother of the suffering servant who is the Son of God, Mary is the figure of the Church, of the community of believers who have been tested in their faith by suffering.[5]

For a long time Christians have been both comforted and perturbed by the thought that in some sense Christ suffered for all and sufficiently for all. They have struggled for centuries to get their minds round the idea that some mysterious suffering has to be endured to put right all the wrong of life and that there was once a young man, not in legend but in history, who went through this enormous pain, watched by his devastated mother and one or two friends.

At the same time the Christian mind has been haunted by the contradictory realization that this sufficiency cannot stand by itself, that there is something lacking, that Christ's suffering needs an extension and completion (Colossians 1:24).

What is lacking in the sufferings of the Jesus of history, which we must fill up, is precisely the incarnation extended in time, what it costs to be a Christian in my place, to be myself but as offered to God for his use. Jesus could only be himself. He was not married, or a soldier, or an artist, or a scientist, or a mother whose child has just been killed in an accident, or a criminal struggling to return to a world that accepts all but criminals, or an old woman of ninety waiting for death and wondering why it does not come— all this is lacking in the archetypal Son of Man who could only be one man. What is lacking in the sufferings of the historic Jesus can be and must be filled up by the sufferings of the body of Christ, the church, as its committed members all become part of his passion. The Eucharist is the sacramental means of repeatedly realizing this and, entering into it, making his passion and his self-offering to God and its price all ours.

In such terms we may understand the Virgin Mary's "Be it unto me according to thy word." The words sum up a process extending over years; they are the theme of a vocation with its sense of being haunted by some huge possibility, as being marked for some unknown glory or responsibility or pain which may make the world quite different from what it is. And the words involve her in keeping this in her heart and brooding on it, drifting between doubt and acceptance continually but holding on to her vision, and still holding on at the foot of the cross.

Mary could have rejected this piercing of the heart. As today someone whom God wants to be a priest, an artist, a teacher, a politician, senses the initial tremors of such a call and considers it and puts it away, so perhaps then there was some other girl who sensed a growing conviction of a special destiny, a desire for an absolute disposability, and in fear at such a summons turned her mind to other possibilities of a happy life. To the mind in meditation the Virgin Mary becomes a type of vocation, the one to whom the extravagant call comes, on whose response a vast amount of the future waits.

It may be said that the Virgin's consent is insignificant compared with that of Christ in Gethsemane, that to Christ's tremendous "yes" any other human "yes" is redundant. Actually it is precisely because Christ's "yes" to God is considered in Christian spirituality as not entirely ours, as in some sense from God, God's act, from outside the human and temporal sphere, that one human being had to consent to being the locus of God's act in time and the human world. Indeed it is an essential part of the Christian view of life that God's saving activity in human history is no more than a dream without innumerable human consents, given again and again in minute particulars.

At the same time this is a joyful mystery in the rosary. Pain as such, without a context of meaning, is sheer misery, but pain within meaning, pain accepted in faith, borne in hope, its ugly head held enclosed in the arms of love, is another thing altogether. Whatever the wreck the storm of pain inflicts on us, let there be a spar of sense to hang on to and we do not drown. The sword piercing Mary's heart is part of the Christian joy.

Chapter 5

THE FINDING IN THE TEMPLE

Jesus was twelve years old when his parents discovered that they had lost him. In St. Luke's story they find him again, but not altogether, because the boy they find is a stranger, saying things they do not understand, moving with a disconcerting confidence in a mental world beyond their reach. His mother did not say much but the situation remained on the edge of her mind for a long time, often distracting her from what she was doing. She struggled to come to terms with it, hampered by memories of the child who for so long had depended on her, fulfilled her by needing her.

Every mother of an adolescent sooner or later realizes that the child she has lived for is lost to her and in his place at the family table is someone who looks like her son but has become something of an enigma. The pain of this realization indicates the extent of the self that must die in her, the possessing, devouring being who longs to be essential to her son. If that self, that mother, does not die in her she will never know the real love of a real son, she will lose him absolutely. If, on the other hand, she is free enough not to need to possess, if she can let him go, let him respond to the call she cannot hear, there will always be the bond of love between them.

Every normal adolescent wants this separation. Growing up means the child gradually finding in himself the authority and wisdom which he previously found in his parents, and it is only when he no longer needs to refer his problems to his parents that he is free to love them. This process is at best never smooth, at worst a continual struggle with hesitations and resistances we only vaguely understand. If the adolescent seeks refuge from the humiliations and problems of life by retreating into the protection of home or of some emotional home-substitute he will never find his own life, he will find even that which he has taken away from him in the sense that the amount of life that he can enjoy will certainly reduce. Since he is not his real self but the creation of his fears, his loving will not be available to him and he will never be able to give his parents or anyone else real love, only his need of support, only his anxiety. If, however, he is lost to his home and is born again into the public world and learns to think and act for himself there, he will be able to meet his father and mother and love them "as himself," as individuals experiencing the problems and pleasures of human existence as he does.

So Jesus' parents lose him when he is twelve years old, and three days later find a son who has gone through the biblical "three days," has died and risen into a new dimension and now speaks about a mysterious concern with God that has taken him and taken him from them. He has begun his own journey into the interior of life.

Everything in life exists for this solitary journey of each individual towards his own grasp of life's meaning and his freedom to love. Marriage itself is for this, to lead husband and wife to their individual experience of life's meaning and their joy in the fullest and most varied loving possible to them. God has willed that they make much of this journey together, find freedom of love to some extent through each other, each the minister of the grace of this sacrament to the other, but marriage is not the goal of their life. Loving is the goal, which means that God is the goal who is himself love and can alone free our loving from all that inhibits it.

This love which is God is infinite love, and the more a husband and wife have of it the more of life they will be able to love. It will enrich what is between them but it will also take them from each other. Because their individual loving has fulfilled each as a self and they have not confined their loving to their marriage, each will have more to give to the other. The more loving they do the more they will be sensitive to the conditions of human life, the universal presence of time in it, of growth, change, and death in it, and they will not see these as enemies but as forms of God's love for us. So Mary and Joseph must not only lose the boy Jesus, Mary must lose Joseph and Joseph must lose Mary again and again in that inner world of God's invitation and man's response whose threshold we always cross alone. They will of course also find one another again and again, but each time to some extent changed. If love holds through all this movement it will be because they choose each other again and again, preferring one another, as each has become, to the rest of the lovable world.

As an image for the life of prayer the lost boy is a symbol of all the losing that has to be gone through by every human being who hopes to make something of the gift of life. We pray to be given the thoughts and desires that will help us negotiate loss—the loss of childhood and youth without secretly being angry that spring should vanish with the rose, without running to defensive pretense or cynicism, without turning against youth because we have lost ours, and so with all our successive losses. There must be some way of acceptance and faith that makes one a good loser. Certainly one suspects that the bad loser does not see his concealed hopelessness which invests one thing after another with life-saving significance so that its going means the end for him. There is a work of identification if we are to find the right response. Many of our losses can be traced to time or our own mistakes, but not all. We may be prone to lose. There is the loss that simply marks the place where the injustice or tragedy of this world broke into our lives.

The religious negotiation of losing turns it into a kind of finding. There is a saying from the Muslim world, "When the heart weeps for what it has lost the spirit laughs for what it has found." A clue to the way in which life might prove this is in the words "How is it that you sought me? Did you not know that I must be in my Father's house?"

"My Father's house" is the place where praise is continually offered to God, where people give thanks for experience, remember the mercy in it, attempt to offer up the still rankling pain, but not without argument—listening and asking within a long tradition of interpreting life in terms of love, God's and man's, and of struggling with the questions raised by this mode of reading experience. Within all that it is discovered that losing and finding belong together and to the goodness of life. We are not to go looking for our lost hour, lost joy, lost love in the company of this world. We are to seek it where it is promised we shall find, within faith in the purpose of God as Jesus understood God, where all lost good is recoverable.

Lost good is recoverable in Christ in the sense that when loss and change are met and lived through by faith they cannot rob life of its meaning or reduce us to being mere victims of what has happened. They become *part of the meaning* in that they are seen, like the rest of experience, as that in which God is believed to express his love. We will not always get a trustworthy hold on so much faith, yet we know that our losses are certainly that in which God is to be trusted and his will done and his peace received. Indeed it is the Christian claim that there is a sense in which, if we see things this way, "in Christ," we just cannot lose (Romans 8:35–39). Prayer is for strengthening this remarkable conviction and increasing the extent to which we live by it. The main purpose of prayer in all mature religion is to develop the hold of its characteristic vision in the believer's mind. It is not what happens but the interpretation we put on it, the way we see it, that decides whether life is a blessing or a curse. So Christianity goes for the *mind* of the Christian, regards the spiritual life as the cultivation of a certain kind of mental life, the "mind that was in Christ Jesus." The essence of this realization is not the monopoly of Christianity or of religion; it figures importantly in the dramas of the psychiatrist's consulting room and indeed wherever people are learning how to cope with experience. To reach it forms one of the great moments of truth. When the principal character in T. S. Eliot's play *The Family Reunion* comes to understand his tragic situation, he is able to say

> ...now
> I feel quite happy, as if happiness
> Did not consist in getting what one wanted
> Or in getting rid of what can't be got rid of
> But in a different vision.

It is part of the Christian vision that everything that happens is within the providence of God and that God can be trusted to help us do his will in everything that happens. The idea accordingly is that one does not settle for one or more particular loves as providing the meaning of life. Meaning does not reside in the person or things loved. The meaning is in fact the loving, and loving more, growing in loving. We grow in love as we see everything within God's love for us and our love for him. St. Augustine describes his struggle to reach this insight as he tried to cope with the havoc in his life caused by the death of his friend, and he concludes:

Blessed is that man that loves Thee, O God, and his friend in Thee, and his enemy for Thee. For he alone loses no one that is dear to him, if all are dear in God, who is never lost. And who is that God but our God, the God who made heaven and earth, who fills them because it is by filling them with Himself that He has made them? No man loses Thee unless he goes from Thee.

Jesus in the temple, questioning the tradition in which he has been brought up, learning and evaluating, is a youth in search of his identity. It is Christian faith that the self matures and is fulfilled, finds itself, by loving. More specifically if we are to be ourselves our love and our aggression need to be so organized that the love in us is free to express itself towards all that is lovable and our aggression is also free to provide energy in the fight against evil. Our success in achieving this is largely determined by the love we received in earliest childhood.

We begin our lives by having only one object of our love and our aggression—the mystery of smiles and frowns and compliance and resistance which is our mother. Through our first knowledge of life, which is our knowledge of her, there is established in us a self that loves her when she is "good" and hates her when she is "bad." The more emotionally intense are our earliest experiences of mother and others the more tangled and knotted are the strands of loving and hating in us in later life. Our loving and hating interfere with each other continually, and the more they do this the more difficult is our task of freeing them for their right objects.

A person who has not known love and security in childhood may later have little ability to experience love except through sex and he will accordingly expect more from sex than it can give. Equally unfortunate is the child who stiffens in the exaggerated security of over-anxious love. The attempt to live within the limits set by parental hopes and needs produces a deep fear of being over-

whelmed which in later years can be detected (often dis-
placed and symbolized) in many of the situations in which
we wish to love but somehow cannot.

We can love with *all* our heart and soul and mind only
when we have been loved with a love that was entirely
happy yet also left us free, in fact with the kind of love
with which Christians say God uniquely loves us all.
However, men are not God. Even their best loving has
never carried the flag so far up the hill of freedom. It is not
possible for any human being to have such an ideal start in
life, so perhaps we can stop expecting people to behave as
though they had and instead try to see within everyone
the wasting lover crying for release.

There is almost nothing recorded of the way Jesus was
loved, what heaven lay about him in his infancy, but it
appears that he knew the security of being loved and the
freedom of being loved by a love that was ready to let him
go. We see him setting out to discover his world and himself as he asks and listens in the temple. Then we lose sight
of him. Years later he comes into our view again, looking
and behaving like a whole person. His love and aggression
are forces of his being that are available to him, they are
not weakened and confused by mutual interference, and
therefore they can be fully and freely offered to God. This
wholeness is bound by the most profound and precious of
all human obligations to what his mother must have been.
From his wholeness we infer her holiness who was star of
his morning and cause of his joy.

Jesus had had love, so he was able to love. St. Paul was
sure that love is greater than faith and hope. One reason
for its priority is that it makes faith and hope possible and
only from faith and hope can new love come. We can love
only if the posture we naturally adopt in the face of experience is an acceptance of life and enthusiasm for it, the
desire to have a real go at it, the assumption that tomorrow need not be disappointment, will certainly be grace,
may even be fun. Ultimately, of course, the greatest of the

three is love because in eternity that is what all will be doing, but in time, here and now, no one can love who has not faith and hope. Without those two flames burning at the center of his existence he is helpless in the grip of a (generally unrecognized) despair and the compulsive appetite for short-term comforts and meanings to keep him going. He must receive; he can only consume life, never produce it. Continually receiving gradually erodes his sense of being the active creator of his life and he loses faith in himself, gives up the task of being himself. Most of what is regarded as sin in the Christian interpretation of life can be traced to this draining away of faith and hope. As Kierkegaard wrote in *Sickness unto Death,* "Sin is: before God in despair not to will to be oneself."

Jesus was free to will to be himself. Mary was fulfilled when she saw that her son no longer needed her and was ready for the world, liked being alive in it, longed to understand it and God's will for it, and already had some tremendous thoughts about this as he went off one day to hear John the Baptist preach—and to meet all the piled-up life waiting to fling itself upon him.

Did he know who he was? How does one know who one is? The answer of religion, which always likes to expand the area of relevance, is that I am one of God's creatures and made in his image. Who is God? The answer Moses got from the bush that flamed with God's presence was "I am who I am." The elusive words can also mean "I will be what I will be." They amount to the deliberate refusal of a name.

Primitive peoples believed that once you knew a god's name you had him in your power. The God who speaks through the burning bush gives Moses no usable name to show that he cannot be used and manipulated by men. The highly charged atmosphere is not forbidding, however, and there is no sign that the presence will withdraw. Martin Buber expounded God's famous reply this way:

God does not make theological statements—but he gives the answer which his creatures need.... That is: You need not cast a spell over me, for I am always with you, as I always choose to be with you; I myself do not assume any of my manifestations beforehand; you cannot learn to meet me, you meet me when you meet me.

In other words, God and the meaning of life and happiness cannot be named in advance, but are discovered in the fullness of the present, in lived situations. It is true of man also that, made in the image of God, he is what he is and will be what he will be. He discovers himself, comes to a sense of identity and aliveness, not by turning a questioning gaze inward at himself but by living intensively in the objective world and responding to its innumerable invitations to discovery and love and endurance. For this intensity of living it is required that we have open minds that do not distort reality by the concealed suspicion that what is coming to us threatens us in some way or by the hidden wish to manipulate it. So James Joyce's main character in *A Portrait of the Artist as a Young Man*, leaving home, writes in his diary:

Mother is putting my new secondhand clothes in order. She prays now, she says, that I may learn in my own life and away from home and friends what the heart is and what it feels. Amen. So be it. Welcome, O life! I go to encounter for the millionth time the reality of experience.

Chapter 6

THE AGONY
IN THE GARDEN

To pray the sorrowful mysteries is to make some attempt to enter the world of suffering. People who say the rosary daily will be considering these dark five twice a week, on Tuesdays and Fridays. Twice a week, however happy or depressed they are, they will bring their perhaps reluctant minds to think about fear, pain, humiliation, the bearing of what must be borne, and death.

There must be some reason for selecting this area of human experience for such frequent consideration that a path is worn smooth through it in the Christian's mental world. It is not because we feel guilty with our surfeit of joy and think we should do some imaginative slumming in the sad world in which the other half lives, much less that we share with secular despair the need to wallow in the unpleasantness of life. It is because suffering so often defeats human beings, is in fact their commonest reason for hating God and life, and we believe Christian faith makes some sense of it.

All the praying that Christians do, the gazings at the crucifix, the endlessly repeated Eucharist are as much for enabling them to take suffering and make use of it as for anything else. The rosary brings five forms of it, taken from the passion of Jesus, before the praying and loving mind. We further particularize by considering some example of each which may be cutting into us or other people just now. This deepens our sense of fellowship with Christ, with Christ in our neighbor and with our neighbor in Christ. It sets this experience of pain within the purpose and presence of God and so gives it a meaning, and one in virtue of which there is something to do with it. There is a limit to what this exercise can do by itself, but along with other means of grace it should make us more sensitive to the pain of the world, its diversity, its disguises (it often wears the mask of the perverse), and it should leave us resolving to relieve it, and aware of our formidable power to add to it.

Such imaginative involvement in the material of prayer is one of the characteristic forms of Christian praying. In eastern religion the aim of prayer seems to be that the believer should progressively feel pain less, and ultimately transcend it, but in this type of Christian prayer the pain of life is set within the purpose of God as revealed in Christ precisely in order to feel it more deeply and to do something creatively with it, to see it not as a soul-hindrance to be surmounted nor a problem to be solved but as a mystery to be lived through in faith.

Pain is certainly a problem for the philosopher and theologian in that they wrestle with it on the intellectual plane and then may come to us with some theoretical pattern in which suffering seems to cohere with the rest of experience, or they offer the judgment that no such softening of the irrationality of pain is possible. It is a "mystery" for the person who prays, and of course for the philosopher as one who prays, in that he lives through it in faith, hope, and love, desiring to know what God wants him to do with it and about it. While he does this he may indeed come to think he understands it a little more but it

is more likely that he will simply come to know more surely that there is no question of not trusting God though the
worst comes to the worst. This "knowledge" is the kind
that comes from living through the mystery; it can never
come from wrestling with the problem.

So the five forms of suffering at the heart of the rosary
do not require a theoretical meditation—they are meant
to be held in a more universal and more personally
involved consciousness. It is this idea that is behind the
artifice of considering all the mysteries of the rosary at first
as through the eyes of the mother of Jesus. In the mind of
the one who prays she is a presence and an attitude. She is
by turns the recalled love, fear, confusion, joy of his mother; she is the representative human sympathy of motherhood, happy, hurt, perplexed, angry; she is also, with all-
inclusive significance, the original and type of anyone who
deeply loves Christ. Because she is all this she is implicitly
and in depth the presence of the church. To meditate the
sorrowful mysteries with her means to set oneself to enter
the world of pain existentially and also to see it with the
faith and thankfulness of the church. It is of the essence of
Christian prayer that what is prayed about is brought into
the light of Christian faith and gratitude. In the rosary this
radiance is poured over each mystery in the repeated words
of the Our Father, the greeting of the Annunciation, the
request for her prayers as the God-bearer, and the *Gloria
Patri*. Certainly the five central mysteries look very different with all that light round them.

On the last night of his life Jesus and his friends had a
meal together that was saddened with the sense of departure and made a thing of fear by the presentiment of death
(Matthew 26:36–56; Mark 14:3–52; Luke 22:40–53). So
much was said and so much, extraordinarily, not said at
that meal that even we who are separated from it by so
many crowded years can feel its enigmatic strain.
Afterwards it appears they walked on the slopes of the
Mount of Olives. In the gathering dusk of his fate Jesus

made no attempt to conceal his distress. In the conflict of emotion he seemed both to want to be alone and to want company; at a place called Gethsemane he withdrew from his friends to pray—to find himself struggling with the longing for their reassuring presence.

It is difficult to decide the details of the mysterious scene that follows. He was alone, yet we know his prayer. There seem to be echoes of the prayer he taught them and us, particularly the phrases "thy will be done" and "lead us not into temptation." There may be elements from the later life of the church. Even so, the vividness of that night-struggle intermittently lit by a shaft of moonlight has impressed generations of believers and unbelievers with its reality and its incommunicable solitude. He seems to have suffered from more than fear, and no one knows what that more was. Whatever it was it shook him to the depths with the sense of this impending onslaught on his integrity. He gropes momentarily for some other way with less searching implications, while his friends (as El Greco depicts them) huddle together in their protective cocoon of compromise and muddle and dream, and then there is the tremendous resolve to go on, to go through.

"All things are possible to thee; remove this cup from me; yet not what I will but what thou wilt." It is probable that Jesus went into Gethsemane believing that the great moment of deliverance, for his people and for him, was soon to come. He believed that it must be preceded by his own suffering, that was how he read the scriptures and life and his own soul, but as the moment approached he began to question what was and what was not necessary to God's purpose, God being understood to love mankind. That his pain was integral to the coming of the kingdom of God was a possibility he could accept. What we think he firm-ly believed was that God would act before the worst came to the worst. The worst, for a man who loved the truth as much as he did, was not something concerning this body that goes down anyway sooner or later. For him the worst was to see the truth murdered, to die for it and with it with no sign that its flag might be raised again. The cry of dereliction on the cross was the shriek of dismay of one for whom the worst has come to the worst. And once again there is the tremendous resolve to go on, to go through. Of course he *must* now; in the last of all our human necessities there is no way out, but it is given to men to go on in trust or rebellion or resignation. He died trusting. "Father, into thy hands I commit my spirit."

This trust does not exclude fear. As any human being he must have feared for himself, what his enemies would do to him, what dying is like. What is more, Gethsemane was by no means his first appointment with fear; he seems to have sensed long before this spectral night that he might lose out all along the line. But for the ultimate, the whole amount of things, the meaning that is not abolished by any of time's ruins but includes them, all his huge soul meant when he said "Abba," "Father," his trust in that held to the end and in the end.

Kierkegaard understood the words "all things are possible to thee" as meaning not that God can do what is impossible, but that if we follow Christ truly, we shall never see the objects of our most intense needs and longings as anything more than possibilities. Nothing is necessary to us except God, not even earthly life (which of course many people have surrendered voluntarily for God's sake and for less), though in our insecurities and their related dependencies we may think we cannot go on without this thing or are afraid to contemplate life without that person. Theologian D. Z. Phillips makes a similar point about overcoming the world:

> But in what sense is it overcome? According to Christianity, it is overcome by a certain kind of love, to possess which is to know God and have eternal life. The believer recognizes that things may not turn out as he would want them to. He must come to terms with that in

such a way that whatever happens he can still go on. He brings his sins, his desires, his expectations to God in prayer, and his wish is that none of these things will come between him and the love of God.

What matters for the Christian is this loving disposition, and the faith and hope that belong to it—so much that it cannot breathe without them, the conviction that these three can survive every wreck. It is this grace that carries God's care for us.

"Pray that ye enter not into temptation." The squad coming to arrest Jesus must have been about three hundred yards away. His friends would soon be running for their lives. The echo of the last petition of the Lord's Prayer suggests that Jesus reminded his friends of the prayer he taught them because this situation was one in which those words would justifiably be on the lips of men who believe in God.

Jesus taught that temptation is to be expected. If he had taught otherwise we should not know what to make of him. There is an ancient extra-canonical tradition that this very night he had already said, "No one can obtain the kingdom of heaven who has not passed through temptation." What men who believe in God may ask of him is not to be spared temptation but to overcome it. In the Lord's Prayer "Lead us not into temptation" means "Preserve us in temptation, do not let us succumb when we are tested."[6] The test referred to may well be the terminal encounter between God and evil which Jesus believed would precede the final coming of the kingdom. In the enormous conflict and confusion of this encounter the faithful would find it hard to distinguish the true from the false, the holy from the unholy.

Whatever the end is, whatever we think Jesus meant by the end, whatever is going to be for each one of us the decisive test, there is a test of our faith that will come many times before the end. It is that hour when in our fear we think some pseudosolution or some form of wrong our savior, or that hour when in our confusion God's face is driven out of our minds and we think we have nothing to believe in.

So we ask God to lead us through such critical experience and out into the light. There is no suggestion that we want one minute of such testing more than is necessary. Indeed, the form of the prayer is shaped out of an egotism somewhat the worse for wear and the suspicion that life could beat us before we are through. It has also grown out of a deep conviction that normally there is no backing out of experience, no getting its value knocked down to you cheap, but that there is a route through the whole tangled, inexplicable thing to what is beyond it, to that state of grace in which we can love the world again, possessing some insight now into where the power and glory of life truly are.

No one can doubt the important role fear plays in every human life, nor how soon it appears. Sometimes it seems that through all our mistakes and unhappinesses can be detected a single thread trailing backwards into our past to some forgotten moment in our childhood when we first felt alone and helpless in a threatening world. Certainly there began then the process of devising ways of avoiding or removing or joining what seems against us so that we can keep going which has in fact kept us going with a wavering dignity until now.

Human beings differ primarily in the efficiency or wastefulness of the techniques they have adopted to keep in the game. Some learn an infinitely precious flexibility of response to life that gives them a marvelous air of freedom and resource, like Jesus, and for this reason they live all their time, get much more life lived than others manage, live what others either evade or never get any further than dreaming. Some hardly ever get it right, and they reduce their chances even further by secretly hoping to produce the impeccable gesture or by accusing others or life or God of being the failure they can no longer bear feeling. All of us through fear have made some too expensive deals with life that mean we shall always meet certain situations at a disadvantage. To acknowledge that this is so is certainly a glimmer of light under the door that stands between us and the possibility of change, between us and God.

It is probable that we fear the world within as much as the world without, especially the accumulations of dismay and anger deposited in our lives as life has flowed by uncaught, unused, carrying so much out of sight. Some of this emotion relates to genuine injury and injustice we have been unable to forgive, some belongs to our earliest experiences of insecurity in childhood when we could not know how you do forgiveness, so that we all have always a quantity of aggression at hand for which we cannot at the moment find a reason. We usually do not suspect its existence until we find ourselves over-reacting in one or other of the ways humans do this, chronic criticizing, irascibility, the phobia, the physical symptom of the tension that is a little easier to bear in the body than it is in the mind. All this means we carry around a self that could, we fear, get the better of us one day.

There is such a thing as habitual fear that we can attempt to reduce, and this is advised in the New Testament (Matthew 6:31–33; Philippians 4:6–7). The deliberate exercise of the will cannot take us very far into the peaceful life but some of the work is to be done this way. It is not that we are anxious on purpose but we occasionally catch ourselves being vaguely satisfied that we are rather more deeply concerned about life than others seem to be, and we notice without perturbation that our friends are a little worried about us. This anxiety has probably slowly grown in us like a bad habit. It could be one of the fifty-seven different ways of dominating.

It pays to see some of the cost of this. The habitually overburdened person is not going to be asked to bear any more, will tend to be omitted from the great communion of helping and being helped which is the love of God, will

have the news withheld when it is bad. Being excluded
from life has nothing to recommend it. There is enough
bitterness to go round and it must go round else some people will break. In order to stand our corner we might aim
at reducing habitual anxiety, even make a small discipline
of the job. If we can manage no meat on Friday, could we
say, to begin with, "no worry on Wednesdays" and see how
this goes? The day has a harmless look of mid-week neutrality that makes it a suitable choice for this modest plan
of personal pacification.

Much more important is the wisdom of practicing forgiveness. There is so much for us all to forgive that we
shall never get it done without putting in a lot of practice.
Every act of forgiveness is a raid on the kingdom of fear.
So if we can forgive more, resent less, we may do a better
job of demolition on our fears. We shall have to work from
the other end as well, of course, and we may not be able to
demolish our deepest fears and angers without help, but
we can practice forgiving life, which is the same as forgiving God. He responds with the gift of peace. The New
Testament calls it with a marvelous flourish the peace
"that passes understanding," which means either that this
peace is worth far more than the fullest understanding of
life by the cleverest of intellectuals or that this peace is a
more effective stabilizer of one's thoughts than any gim-
mick human wit could think up.

Every fear-situation is an encounter with God. It may
never look like this but it is worth remembering that we
have never exhaustively sorted out what it means to meet
God. He can be answering prayer in our reverses and very
doubtfully present when our wishes are met. That is simply a cautionary way of pointing up our ability to misread
situations. God is of course always present, in the best and
the worst, can never be anything but present. In the experience of fear, the Christian differs from the unbeliever not
in that he has some reason to expect that the cup may pass
from him but in his certainty that if it does not pass it

comes to him ultimately from the hand of God who is with him to the last drop. He may cry out that he is forsaken, but the sense of being forsaken is part of his experience of God's presence at such a time. That is how God is near. Philosopher Simone Weil is an illuminating observer of this profound coherence of pain and faith in the Christian life. We know, she writes,

> that joy is the sweetness of contact with the love of God, that affliction is the wound of this same contact when it is painful, and that only the contact matters, not the manner of it.... The knowledge of this presence of God does not afford consolation, it takes nothing from the fearful bitterness of affliction, nor does it heal the mutilation of the soul. But we know quite certainly that God's love for us is the very substance of this bitterness and this mutilation. I should like out of gratitude to be able to bear witness to this.[7]

The Christian life is more than enduring. Something has to be done in and with what has to be endured, and a grace received from God for this doing. Without anxiety, and with gratitude, we are to ask what God's will is and be ready to learn. Believers find that through this kind of openness and honesty and trust the senseless situation takes on meaning, becomes endurable for that reason; they are given a more productive view of their difficulties, they abandon certain mistaken expectations about them. It does not often happen in this world that a problem is fully solved. There are improvements, clearings, loosenings, so that after some standstill movement becomes possible again. Occasionally, for all our insight and effort and the grace received, things seem to deteriorate, but only seem. It all depends on the principle of measurement. Do we think Christ was in fact forsaken? We do not. We believe he entered into the only kingdom that matters, the kingdom of love and truth, and we do not care who forgets us if we are remembered there.

Chapter 7

THE SCOURGING

The trial and conviction of Jesus are given unusually detailed description in the New Testament so that we have more than a glimpse of that bit of history, the competing interests, the fears and the lies, the general ignorance of the issues, and the way in which all these factors penetrate and influence judicial procedure. Even so, it is not all clear—it happened a long time ago, and the records themselves have come down to us from a profoundly interested party, the followers of the condemned man. What is perfectly clear is that Jesus aroused the fear and therefore the violence of the world.

There is a degree of peace and equilibrium that society must maintain or else things fall apart. The process of law is part of the elaborate structure man has erected against that which threatens his peace. It is man's attempt to cope rationally with disturbers of the peace by regulating both aggression and the private and public reaction to aggression. It is in this sense a product of fear, fear of the enormously destructive power which individuals and groups carry within them. The fear of violence operates violently, as the history of penal customs revoltingly shows. How Jesus approached this area of life and was drawn into its hideous center can be traced in the gospels in considerable detail. In the prayer of the many Christians who use the rosary this part of Jesus' life is summarily represented by the brutality of the scourging. The selection of such an uncompromising image suggests a penetrating recognition that it is impossible to follow Jesus without having one's eyes opened to the fact of violence.

In the Eucharist, before the great thanksgiving at its center, the congregation makes a deliberate affirmation of its peace of mind, its mutual reconciliation, and its reconciliation with life. The authority for this is Jesus' view that the unreconciled mind cannot make the offering of praise and thanksgiving (Matthew 5:23–24). The main disturber of our peace is our estrangements and hostilities, and the management of these is an essential part of praying.

The strongest of our constitutional energies is that provided by the drive of aggression. It is always much more easily released than any wisdom we may acquire, but by this power man has survived the innumerable threats of the evolutionary struggle. Without it he would scarcely last a day. It is still true that when he is afraid he must in a sense either hit or run. Today man needs this energy in his struggle against all that threatens what is good in his world, and for his effort to extend the range of present good and to make new good. Every individual is involved in saying "Yes" to one thing and "No" to another every day of his life and needs the power to assert himself so far.

This alternation of Yes and No works out for many people in a sense of the worthiness of life, but for many others in the conviction that things have mostly been against them and mostly are.

When things go badly for us in our childhood the resentment we feel can rarely be expressed and discharged. It seems it does not fade away but is stored up in the mind, the sinister savings of infancy, often to no very great inconvenience in later years, but if it is intense it has to be forcibly repressed and so acquires an explosive character.

Resentments in adult life may well activate this earlier aggression and so increase the range of the resenting self. We may not understand that this is happening, we are certainly not responsible for the fear and aggression originating in childhood, but if we understand this situation it becomes part of the inner revolt we must come to terms with now.

If we are keen to make progress in the enjoyment of life there are always chronic or temporary disappointments, frustrations, personal inconsistencies with which we must cope. We do not do this work as successfully as we (sometimes unjustly) think we ought. We begin to be ashamed of ourselves and feel we do not add up to much.

Current resentment at life, reinforced by the stored-up protest of childhood, intensified by a poor view of oneself amounts to a weight of hostility that is itself rather frightening and is certainly more than we can bear. Christian believers are particularly disturbed when they begin to suspect the extent of the aggression that fumes within because of the taboo on anger in the teaching of Jesus. This taboo has been traditionally interpreted in a lethally legalistic way. It seems that Jesus' main concern was with the honest recognition of negative emotion as a primary condition of its transformation into something more useful. To inculcate shame and fear in relation to our aggressiveness, in the name of Jesus, is to misunderstand his method. Christians nevertheless have this hypersensitiveness to their rage at things and are the more likely to be unable to acknowledge it.

What we cannot bear to look at in ourselves we inevitably project onto the world which we now see in an increasingly menacing light. We blame others for the faults we cannot bear to admit in ourselves, we are critical of those who have the happiness or success we secretly curse ourselves for not reaching, we are furious with others for not reaching the perfection we unconsciously and tyrannically demand of ourselves, we chastise the church for not being successful enough to reassure us nor saintly enough to inspire us.

This is why there is always someone being scourged, someone suffering to satisfy the general guilt and hostility. This is what this mystery of the rosary is about—our hostility to things, our fear of its destructive power, and the way we recover a kind of peace by discharging this aggression in the chastisement of life.

Most of this is not deliberate at all, at any rate not conscious. People usually do not notice for long enough how intense their disappointments are, how excluded from life they feel, how certain they are that they are not now going to pull out of this grey weather into the sunlight. To realize this would probably be more of a meal of reality than they can stomach. So they see their pains as injuries. When this happens we secure a kind of peace, but only a kind. It is something like the shamefaced interval secured by postponing uncongenial work we ought to be doing now. The identification of the supposed source of our injuries brings a kind of intellectual satisfaction. To attack it gives us a kind of triumph, a small revenge. This process is widely diffused throughout human life, indeed wherever the disappointed and angry mind that will not look within finds a kind of peace in victimizing people, life, or God. This is what the Christian attempts to get his mind round when he brings into his prayer the image of the pillar where Christ stands and bleeds.

We believe that the Jesus who cannot protect himself from the blows of the world's malevolence is not merely man. We can see at any rate that much of our hostility towards life and people is really our disapproval of the way things are. Ultimately it is God who is responsible for this and much of our hostility is really meant for him. It is to God's creative act that we trace the fact that our world is this kind of a world, one in which human beings are free to be wonderful and horrible, are subject to dangers they cannot control, make material and spiritual progress through various kinds of success and failure, must all sooner or later die. It is not the case that many people consciously reject this state of affairs but there is a strict limit to how much of it they will accept. When our disappointments, shocks, failures exceed a certain total we smell injustice in the air. If our objection advances beyond the item of pain under which we suffer to the conditions themselves under which human life is lived (particularly its inherent possibility that everything could go wrong), our wrath is aimed at God. Sometimes we express this by refusal to believe in him, though generally that refusal to believe is merely a disguise for the running fight we are having with him.

It is worthwhile looking at our reason for fighting him. Not many of us have a very clear idea of what a better arranged world than this one would be. All depends on what we think life in this world is for. Can anyone seriously think it is for happiness—in the sense of the mere satisfaction of one want after another? It certainly does not look like that. It looks as if for the greatest number of people it is the worst of all possible worlds for that.

The Christian view is that life in this world is for the learning and practicing of faith and love and that it represents only a fraction of the opportunity for this that God intends us to have. The rest will be given us in a further range of life beyond this world, and it will culminate in an infinity of faith and love which will make all our tears now look like misunderstandings.

For this reason the Christian assumes and looks for a special meaning, deeper than mere happiness yet consistent with life's purpose, in every human life, however joyful, however wretched. It is always related to the blessedness of knowing and loving God in people and things, in the good and the bad. "God has made us for blessedness—and we grope wretchedly for happiness. Happiness is the thing we first think of and want. It is unworthy of us, and our deepest self rejects it. Blessedness is God himself."[8]

To ask "Why should this happen to me?" when calamity or illness strikes one implies a view that is not worthy of a rational human being, namely, that it should have happened to someone else, someone who one thinks deserves it, or that it should not have happened at all. To think that there is some just balance between virtue and freedom from misfortune and that this is how the love of God functions is to be in a different mental world from that in which Jesus lived and loved. The teaching of Jesus is that there is little evidence that God rewards the good and punishes the wicked in this world; the rain falls on the unpleasant man's field as abundantly as it does on that of his exemplary neighbor, the sun shines as brightly for the one as for the other; there is much in life that you cannot alter and must accept with as much equanimity as you can summon, and it is easier to do this if you do not try to live faster than time, if you avoid adding tomorrow's load onto today's. He had the clearest view of the insecurity and pain of life, saw these with an additional sharpness because at a very early stage he felt he was singled out for a special involvement in the outrageousness of things, yet he never doubted the power and the justice and the love of God. He did not think he had any claim on God for an explanation of suffering, because he did not think man has any means of judging what is fitting and what is not fitting for God, but he believed that God is to be trusted.

This trust, which is the clue to the Christian religion, does not derive from the belief that God has undertaken to see that his trusting children fare well in this life but from the conviction that life is *for* coming to know God through responding in faith and love to his claiming, blessing, wounding presence as it encounters them in every situation. If Christians are right in this understanding of Christ and life things begin to take on a new look. The world looks as though it could indeed have been made for learning and practicing faith and love. It might even be said that it is the best of all possible worlds for that.

This is not to say that the Christian, secretly armed in his optimistic worldview, does not feel the mystery of pain as much as others who interpret life in more melancholy terms. There is no evidence that people who have a grim view of life are particularly sensitive. Indeed, there is often a disguised comfort and narcotic in the depressed view. One of the common neurotic escapes from reality is to lose oneself in a general misery and hopelessness in order to lessen the sting of some particular pain. The Christian aim is the harder thing—to be alive to as much of life as possible, to its sorrow as well as its joy.

This means that he cannot allow himself the relief of dealing with the problem of evil by viewing it in some cosmic perspective in which it disappears at some intellectual vanishing point. That would be to attempt to solve the problem by dismissing it. The believer is not called to solve the problem of evil at all but to live with the mystery of it in faith and love. "Living with" means not just viewing, it means feeling, sharing, understanding, and striving to amend, if only in part, each evil situation, and believing that your labor is not in vain in the Lord.

The ultimate Christian trust will sharpen the anguish and enigma of each situation that challenges it as well as make it endurable. This is why prayer must include such brutal images as the scourging. To face and feel the pain of the world is to consider the fear and resentment which lie behind its infliction, and it is to remind oneself how often in human aggression the victim stands for some hated part of the tormentor's self or is simply the lay figure for someone's denunciation of life. By doing this exercise we do not understand evil much more but we make room for pity in our attitude to it. The time it takes to come so far in sensitiveness is worth it.

A further step to be taken is to acknowledge that these twin streams of fear and resentment flow through our own lives as well as the lives of others. Some of our fears and hostilities are justified and require appropriate action, some of them are in excess of the situation, and some conceal themselves from us, but the more we examine them sincerely, wanting to understand, instead of just airing our hostilities in a flow of habitual complaint and accusation, the more alive and hopeful we feel about ourselves and therefore less interested in attacking others or life. We fly at whatever we think is our enemy in part, in considerable part, from self-contempt.

Occasionally we experience evil as unqualified injury, when we meet the inescapable tragedy of life or suffer some person's cruelty. It is possible then to overcome evil with good. There are fewer chances of doing this than we think.

Evil is rarely, if ever, sheer malevolence. Usually bad luck and ignorance and a second-rate psycho-physical constitution combine to expose in the sinner some area of the weakness which we all carry, either guiltily or with unconvincing nonchalance. And good is never pure good in this world, it is always the imperfectly good, the best perhaps that could be done in the circumstances, but always mixed with some degree of self-regard.

When sheer evil is done to us we have the rare chance of overcoming evil with good. We overcome evil with good by not letting it degrade us. If we receive it into ourselves and do not let it weaken our desire to do God's will, that part at any rate of the vicious circle of sin and retaliation is broken. We also virtually wipe out half of that person's sin, the part that consists in damage done to others. To do this is to become one of the places where evil is being turned into good. If it is the impersonal wrongness of circumstance, some part of the human tragedy that strikes us, we are presented with an equally rare opportunity of showing, whoever may be glad to see this, that we truly love God. "When we love God through evil as such, it is really God whom we love."[9]

When people think in this way it is astonishing how the tables are turned on the evil of life. It is well known that in the concentration camps, along with the humiliations, the suicides, the defeat of what we call humanity, there were extraordinary triumphs of the spirit.

This prayer was found written on a piece of wrapping paper in Ravensbruck, the largest of the concentration camps for women, when it was freed:

> O Lord, remember not only the men and women of good-will but also those of ill-will. But do not remember all the suffering they have inflicted on us; remember the fruits we bought, thanks to this suffering, our comradeship, our loyalty, our humility, the courage, the generosity, the greatness of heart which has grown out of this; and when they come to judgement, let all the fruits that we have borne be their forgiveness.

Chapter 8

THE CROWNING
WITH THORNS

Jesus' road to death was diverted for a while through a series of humiliations devised round the theme of a mock king. Blindfolded, a soldier's cloak put round his shoulders as a robe, a reed in his hand as a scepter, a ring of twigs from a thorn-bush as a crown, he received the ridicule and mock homage of the palace troops, and, as this figure of exposed and humiliated man, he has haunt-ed the Christian mind ever since.

The soldiers may have been doing more than appears in the written account. There are mysterious parallels to their treatment of Jesus in ancient rituals connected with the need to replenish the vitality of the land at the end of winter and to maintain the strength of the community through the person of its royal head. The significance of these primitive parallels is not identifiable now, though they will always excite speculation, but the hold which the mocking of Jesus has on the imagination may owe some of its power to the less obscure fact that it is an image of the alienated spirit.

This range of experience has always been familiar country to the artist. In the poems of Baudelaire, in the paintings of Toulouse-Lautrec, Rouault, and Picasso, the anguish of alienation is repeatedly expressed—often in the image of a circus character, especially the clown (sometimes with additional bitterness the ageing clown) who is at the mercy of the world's dubious approval, compelled to play a role, inwardly isolated because always misunderstood, unable to be his true self. Today, however, this outsider, the man out of accord with his time, is the commonest character in the serious work of the international cinema, television drama, and the novel, because today anyone who thinks and feels sooner or later finds himself alone, wondering whether it is he who is mad or the rest.

Human beings will have to face mockery, insensitiveness, exposure until the end of time. When we are humiliated we are usually driven to compensate, we must hurt someone else because we have been hurt, or find some other way of dissipating the sense of being despised. Our Lord chose another way out. He remained in control, accepting it all, and perseveringly made the humiliations part of his triumph. The passion of Jesus bears the meaning he gave to it, not theirs who caused it. All that he went through he made part of his offering to God, so that it becomes the type of offering at its best, the true sacrifice, the gift that is made in faith and love and leaves God to do with it what he wills to make of it.

There are people who do not now see Jesus with this light around him. They feel he has lost his appeal, is not taken very seriously now, is beginning to look much less important; his claim to be the Son of God seems somewhat pretentious, almost ridiculous. It is part of the life of faith to have to deal with such dismaying thoughts, to reply to the inner voice that suspects the whole thing is a kind of game. The image of a ridiculous Christ is for the strengthening of faith under that stress. It is a highly dramatic reminder that we live by faith. We are on the wrong lines if we look for something about Jesus that makes it clear that he is God, so that having identified that feature we know who he is and know that there is no risk to the amount of personal capital we have invested in him. The truth is that in this world we are never going to *know* that he is king. Sometimes he is going to *look* quite absurd.

The figure of the humiliated and ridiculed Christ leads the praying mind into a wide range of human suffering whose pain is all the greater for its being usually private and lonely. The person whose sympathies are formed in this way will become increasingly sensitive to all people who have to endure seeing their deepest convictions made to look foolish; to those whom life or their own fault has forced into doing the opposite of what they really want to do, who feel that they are just playing a part and long for the opportunity to be real; to all those who feel there is no one at all who understands. The mind that is used to recalling how they blindfolded Jesus and struck him and asked him to identify his attacker may well see this situation repeated in the lives of those whose personal problems spring from disturbances in the subconscious mind so that in a sense they too are blindfolded and cannot see where their suffering is coming from and only know that each day they find reality more hateful. Christ is exposed in all whose secret shame or love has been found out, whose self-revelation is received casually or brutally, who lose the things that gave them identity and sheltered them—like the widow going into the old people's home who must sell up and go in without the bits and pieces that represent her past and indeed her self since she is mostly now a past.

Many of our humiliations are not circumstantial. We construct them ourselves or at least invite them by misguided choices in our way of living life. There are certain situations to which we are unwilling to risk exposure. The most important of these situations is the pain of failure. In our anxiety to avoid this pain we often adopt an over-optimistic view of ourselves as beings who ought not to fail, ought to be "Christian," do not have unrecognized hates or exaggerated expectations of people.

The attempt to live up to such a view of ourselves causes endless trouble. It conceals from us both our limitations and our assets, to say nothing of our need of God. The result is that we go into life unwilling to face ourselves and therefore unable to know ourselves. We must function neither in the Holy Spirit nor in truth. To be "in the Spirit" is to want to know and do God's will and in his strength and in his time, not to be driven by our merciless egos. To be in the truth is to live according to the facts and not according to our fantasies.

The more we avoid the facts and attempt to appear other than we are the more we dread situations in which the truth may be revealed. This fear can take such a hold of its victim that he has to withdraw from much of life lest this situation or that should enable the world to behold the man, the man he is.

We may even reach the condition, which Jesus so graphically described (Matthew 25:14–30) of seeing life as a hard and unreasonable affair in which the impossible is expected of us. We imagine ourselves failing in everything. We cannot expose ourselves to such continued humiliation.

Sooner or later, however, we must necessarily run into a different kind of humiliation—of having a lot of unlived life on our hands because we hid what we could have given, buried what we might have risked.

Even so, there could be positive gain in this. If we can find out how much we ourselves contribute to our humiliating situations with our exaggerated fears and expectations, we shall at any rate have that bit of liberating truth in our possession, that bit of the Holy Spirit making things easier.

The truth is that each one of us from infancy onwards develops in a double fashion. There is, in theory, the self we naturally strive to become, would become if our experience was a uniformly smooth and reasonably successful development. We do in part become this self, but from early days inevitable rebuffs and failures produce the suspicion that this self is in various ways not acceptable. There follows the unconscious erection of an image of the self as we think we ought to be, must be if we are going to get by. We despise and reject the real self because we cannot bear to think that that unsatisfactory and humiliated creature is us. We prefer to see ourselves in terms of this ideal self because we believe it is going to be acceptable and successful, but we are not absolutely certain of this, and so we begin to need to convince ourselves and be convinced by life that it is this ideal self that is us.

We have to employ a great variety of twists and turns to avoid confronting the fact that we are not measuring up to our ideal. We deny the thoughts and feelings that are inconsistent with what we want to be and think we ought to be. We avoid admitting faults by condemning them in others who fail as we do or by attacking some other form of the universal human failure as a substitute. When these ruses fail and we cannot avoid recognizing our culpability we explain it away as the result of some handicap for which we are not responsible. We may take refuge in some compensatory superiority (however superficial) that will elevate us in our own or others' regard, or drive ourselves forward under the lash of perfectionism or run to the final funk-hole of despair. These strategies are little use to us. We merely part company with reality, and we certainly suffer more than we need.

The life of faith is among other things a way of getting oneself off one's back. The self I think I ought to be and the self I want to be may be quite different, and both may be against the interests of my real self in the sense that each could be part of a misguided attempt to reach some kind of personal and social acceptability.

The Christian view is that we can never know with any confidence what we ought to be or what we want to be. In Christ man is seen as a being of freedom and love and honesty and peace. The believer is one who is excited by that revelation to pursue what it may mean for him in the community of those similarly excited and summoned. As he is drawn further in and begins the journey of faith he finds life presenting a friendlier and more trustworthy appearance, finds himself beginning to think it could all mean love in one sense or another. This is enough to go the rest of the way with.

On this journey we learn the necessity of demolishing many of our ideas of what we ought to be. Such dreary moralistic categories may indeed become meaningless in the only world that matters—the world of those who have seen the love and freedom and God-centeredness of Christ as defining what being human truly is. To them the manhood of Christ is something they love and want. As they understand it more they realize they had burdened themselves with a set of standards they thought they ought to reach but now what matters is desiring and loving, and what is desirable and lovable. What we wanted to be (admirable, successful, invulnerable) begins to fade in the attraction of what he is, as candle-flames fade in the sun.

This does not mean the end of humiliation. It means the end of the humiliation that depresses and the beginning of a power to use humiliation so that it becomes productive. One of the deepest and most fascinating of the Christian ideas is that of humility. There is certainly no progress in humility without humiliation. Our failures all have to be faced sooner or later. It is the Christian conviction that they are faced without depression and within a huge hopefulness as we "learn Christ" because the experience of being a failure is incidental to a life which is a matter of simultaneously learning love and discovering grace. In such a life there is an infinite hopefulness about all confessed failures because they are opportunities of discovering more about what love is and who God is and how his mercy persists in turning the most revolting material to good.

This extremely sensitive area of the life of faith has such possibilities of spiritual hang-up as well as spiritual growth that the use of sacramental confession and some form of spiritual direction is almost essential. The aim is not only to see our failures more clearly but to see them where we did not suspect their presence. Yet we interpret them productively, not in terms of some success/failure ratio of the secular world but in the mercy of Christ as the ignorant and frightened price we pay for insulating ourselves from love and ensuring the restricted survival we have so foolishly settled for.

In the new life the Christian has chosen to live in Christ he fails continually. All of these failures will be failures in loving; in Christ there is really no other kind. Some of them will be sins to be confessed; but at no time is he to consider himself the contemptible being that has haunted his depressions in his graceless days. That contemptible self was merely the creation of his early rejections and unacceptability. It is as exaggerated as the ideal self he has by compensation tried to believe in and reach, only to plunge further into humiliation because it was so necessary to him to reach it.

It is part of the sanity of Christ that with him as guide success and failure are normal and expected and the one should not lift us too high nor the other throw us too hard; and the only successes and failures really worth attention are those in loving. Even so all is within a realm in which God's presence invites and his power enables and his forgiveness is the stimulus of a fresh start that never loses its freshness however often it is so compassionately given us. Eventually we come to see that everything is grist to the mill of the spiritual life, that there is a fascinating question mark over all that is normally called success and failure, and that there is a growing life of thankfulness and commitment within us that is much more important than either success or failure. It is a very great mercy to be lifted out of the exhausting alternation of unrealistic self-contempt and equally unrealistic self-esteem.

Through thankfulness and commitment to God and man the true self is made. What it will ultimately be is a mystery. All we know is that it is in the making. The Christian attitude is made clear in the first letter of St. John (1 John 3:2) where it is pointed out that we know now what it is to see life as proceeding from a divine fatherliness. What the future holds we do not know except that if we go on with this life of thanking and giving we shall know more of what it is to be man as Jesus was man.

It is said that when the soldiers finished fooling about with Jesus, finished using him for whatever purpose drove their slow and simple minds, they stripped him of the paraphernalia they had put on him and dressed him in his own clothes again. He went to his tremendous end as himself, and we do not know what he looked like then. The most detailed description of his appearance in the gospels is of a fabricated Jesus, a figure set up for someone's use. The essential Christ is less clear. This is a sign for us that the spiritual life is not an emulation, not an imitation, which can only lead either to pride or to despair, but a living in the love of God as it is mediated to us in the calls, supports, rebukes, forgivenesses, longings, companionship of that realm of grace which is the holy catholic church, which, in spite of its interminable fooling around with things that are not the center of the matter, in spite of the sad declining of its majesty, remains the one and only group that remembers Christ with gratitude and longing and must go on doing just that because it will be responsible if his name should perish from the earth.

Chapter 9

THE CARRYING
OF THE CROSS

In the world in which Jesus lived, when condemned criminals were marched to the place of their execution they were made to carry the cross on which they were to die. Jesus was unable to sustain the whole of this gruesome journey, probably because of extreme exhaustion, but he endured it to the limit of his strength, and then someone else was compelled to take over (John 19:17; Luke 23:26–32).

Because the minds of his friends who saw this or heard about it were so deeply scarred by the horror of his helpless stumbling to his place of death, or because he suffered a fate in such revolting contradiction to his nature as the Word through whom the world was made, the carrying of the cross seems to have become very quickly one of the essential and dramatic ideas of the Christian life.

Jesus himself is said to have used it in his teaching (Luke 9:23), though the origin of this saying may have been the preaching of the early church rather than the teaching of Jesus. Even so it is probable that it did not carry literally the idea of death (there is little evidence that many Christians were in fact crucified) but became a pregnant metaphor for the political danger and social ostracism the Christian convert might expect to suffer. It was then absorbed in the dying-to-live imagery that became such a characteristic form of Christian understanding of the life of faith.

If we use the language of Christ's passion for our own experience of pain it can only be with a certain reserve. Some pain, even though intense, cannot be described in terms of the formidable and mysterious pain that has haunted the Christian imagination all these years. Pain is everywhere and infinitely various but not all of it is in any way a form of the cross of Christ. The thousand natural shocks that flesh is heir to are not the cross. They deserve man's sympathy and God's, if God exists, but the king of glory does not die on them.

Christ suffered for his ideas, not because he was arthritic or neurotic or illegitimate or spastic or through any form of pain that he could not avoid. It is essential to the Christian understanding of the cross that Christ need not have ended his short and apparently not unhappy life there. He had to end it there because of the free decisions into which his freely chosen understanding of life led him.

There have always been people whose decision for Christian faith involved them in intense suffering, and there are such today, but there are many for whom that decision has resulted in their lives being so much better organized and rescued from so many mistaken and wasteful methods of dealing with experience that they would want to describe it in the language of joy.

Even so, most of us wish we had made better use of existence than we have yet done and hope that Christ will help us to do this before our sands run out. There are frustrations and disappointments in every life. Many lives have to be lived with the never-ending injustice of things. The Christ who carries his cross as far as he can becomes identified in the praying mind with all who suffer under the weight of emotional, economic, political burdens and become in this way a million places of the real presence of God. There, at any rate, he emerges from his traditional obscurity and can be clearly seen and served.

Christians struggling with necessity and limitation in their own lives, with that which simply has to be borne, have drawn a kind of comfort and stamina from the thought of Christ under the weight of his cross, hearing his unresenting groans alongside theirs, though it is alarmingly easy to use Christ's pain merely as a picture of our own. We are less likely to run this considerable spiritual risk if we also use the more general contemplation of Christ and his cross as the image of the dying of the false and immature self that we must undergo so that our real self, as God intends us, may come to life. Some of this has to be done daily if we are Christians, and some of it hurts, but it is accepted and endured more easily if we think of the joy that is set before us, the freedom and loving that in Christ form the image of life's huge possibility.

We find our way to that freedom and love by living the thousand lonely mistakes of egotism and ignorance and taking the consequences and asking if things needed to be so much of a let-down and looking at Christ. In such moments we learn that a compact with God should put beyond reach what his enemy might give us to enjoy, that only one kind of person is ever going to inherit the earth, that knowing and accepting one's limitations is part of becoming that kind of person.

The limitations are what we cannot do, what we ought not to do though we can, what we may not ask God to do. They concern what we cannot know. There is much that we cannot know for sheer lack of time; we must be willing to leave life not knowing most of what is obviously marvelously worth knowing. We cannot have it all. And these limitations concern what we cannot know because God does not mean us to know it in advance, like the future and whether we are going to pull through.

The limitations of life are not depressing, because over against them is the world of the limitless, the inexhaustible self under grace, the ability to sense beauty and make it, to see where suffering hides and relieve it, to tie things together in meaning, to love and be grateful, indeed to be all that is valid forever and can be used in the unimaginable variety and abundance of experience that God is saving up for us.

That next-world fulfillment is not a compensation for the limitations of this world which become tolerable because of the brightness ahead. It is not the case that all human limitations are disadvantages, or injustices, to be approached resentfully or defensively; they are the form in which life comes and if they are lived with and through, undistorted by our fears and preconceptions, we shall find that far more can be done with them and gained from them than by fighting them. The more life we allow into our experience the more likely we are to find it good. If we want to reduce the amount and variety of our life it must be that we are frightened of it, or are cryptosuicides, disgusted or furious with it.

Sometimes we are justified in being disgusted with life or made angry by it. We then need our maximum of emotional freedom and courage for assessing the situation and taking such action as is open to us for changing it as it seems God wills it to be changed. If we find there is nothing we can do, or do just now, or that our previous efforts are having no success, the life of faith will then take the form of acknowledging our helplessness or failure there and turning to some other part of experience.

Failure is as much a part of life as success is and by no means something in front of which one sits down and howls as though it is a scandal and a shame. To live spiritually is to live in the truth, registering the facts of life with the anger, disgust, amusement, questioning, pleasure, reverence they deserve and learning how much of these the various facts are worth.

Some examples of what must be borne in this life are so appalling that one cannot avoid the feeling that only the victims should be allowed to speak of them, these alone being exempt from the suspicion of drama, but it is frequently observed that most of the truly doomed are silent on their special subject, finding other things to talk about. Yet all faiths are committed to attempting to make sense of life. The Christian attempt involves the view of this world as the real but very imperfect setting for our learning how to trust and love both God and man and discovering what such faith and love can do with life.

Within this scheme, all that for the time being has to be borne is seen as a sign keeping before men's eyes the reality and imperfection of things, and therefore as a cry for help. Sometimes the sufferer's faith and love, and the faith of those near him, are so impressive that suffering may also be seen as another sign, of the way in which life's grossest limitations are themselves limited and in certain spiritual conditions become transparent, letting so much of the kingdom of God through that people are driven seriously to wonder who actually are the winners and who the losers in life.

This transformation of suffering so that much of its evil is turned into good is possible only when it is accepted, as any other part of life, to be lived through with God and for God in faith that he will use it in some part of his purpose. The individual concerned can rarely do all of this. Others will be to some extent involved. In some cases (the autistic or spastic child, the psychotic, the senile), others must do almost all the accepting, and what comes of that. They become people compelled to carry the cross on the *via dolorosa* of life. This itself is part of the purpose of God who seems to want us giving to and receiving from one another at such depth and in such complication that ultimately all will be full of gratitude and all will see how needed they were.

Acceptance is not resignation, which is a dead end in the sense that it has no life about it and nothing comes from it. Christian acceptance is a beginning. It is the taking up of a position preliminary to action, and the best possible position, since it is the concurring of the will with things as they are at the moment, preparatory to attempting to find what God wants us to do with the situation. The concurring of the will means that the mind will be free, not tightly organized by resentment or fear but able to put the whole of itself into the fight or the work, able to use what it has already learned about life, and adaptable too, open to guidance, ready to change habitual attitudes that will not work this time, as it feels its way to discernment of the right course.

It is often harder to bear with oneself than with any frustrations in one's circumstances, though this may be simply a matter of turning against ourselves the disapproval of life that for some reason we cannot express. More often we find ourselves a burden through our unacknowledged wish to be rather successful spiritually; we are driven to exasperation with ourselves through the shame of being continually tripped up by contemptibly ordinary failures in tolerating people and putting up with life's frictions. We may then resort to hopelessness and cynicism about the life of faith, or we become sanctimonious Christians, unpleasantly ready to wear our spiritual inadequacy on our sleeve, or we externalize in good works in which the love of God has completely disappeared in the agitated service of our unfortunate neighbors, or we throw in the towel and quit.

Everyone has to cope with the self's need to expand and gain power, with its variable success and its consequent fantasies of importance and inferiority. We need reassurance as keenly as the body needs food. For this reason much of the time our egocentricity or our immaturity is showing, and we have to live with this fact. It is part of the Christian life to get used to being a rather unsatisfactory self. It is all never really going to come right in time.

Some people use the sacrament of penance as though it gives them a new self. That is a romantic view. There is a sense in which that wonderfully restoring and necessary sacrament wipes the slate clean, but it is of the guilt of the evil past, not of the self. Even if it is granted that guilt is a quality of actions, and therefore something that can be completely forgiven, it usually relates to an orientation of the wanting self, which remains and must cause more sin, until its unwisdom is clearly seen and it is abandoned for a more efficient one. It looks as if we are meant to be stuck with ourselves forever, but there is the chance of progress, and the situation is not without a touch of humor. Freud is reported to have said to a patient, "I'm afraid we can't cure your hysterical misery but we will try to turn it into ordinary human unhappiness."

Within this ineluctable self achievement and failure mix uncertainly, are sometimes present together, but underneath is the possibility of surrender, the ability to give oneself in love as completely as something thrown into the sea. Life for the Christian is learning how to do that, clearing the way for that giving. We only truly exist by giving love, but we have to acquire this power, by learning how to love things so that we can love people and how to love people so that we can love God. This learning means in part to fail, but whatever we do that has love in it God works into his larger scheme. It will appear at length in its true place and significance where small and great, first and last, Christ says, do not have the anxious meaning we give them in the world of vanity and fear. To love means to love and make mistakes and have doubts and to be overcome by evil sometimes and to be vulnerable always, and it means to live with all this and through it because loving is living in a certain way; it is not a mere part of one's living, one of several interests, like oil-painting which you give up when you find you are not going to do it very well or you cannot afford the latest increase in the price of paint.

The amount of life that has to be borne is not distributed evenly or in proportion to the ability to bear. Many people are breaking, many could bear more. It is obvious that there must be extensive giving and receiving of help. Christ had to be helped with his cross. Christians normally have no difficulty with the need to give help but they are often incapable of receiving any. This desire to be more Christian than Christ is the presenting sign of a compulsive attempt to find security through self-sufficiency. It conceals the hurt soul's fear of life, of being so closely involved in its many relationships that one would come into the dangerous condition of needing.

The emphasis on "unselfishness" in traditional Christian teaching is partly responsible for this. It is not always more blessed to give than to receive, though many Christians have been persuaded by earnest mentors to twist their reluctant minds into thinking that it is. There are many points of the spiritual life at which the more blessed thing is to receive love and it is the more difficult thing. There is not much heard about this in Christian preaching nowadays, today's preaching being so mournfully weighted with altruism, but it has its due place in the literature of Christian prayer and in the novel and the theater. Henry James was deeply sensitive to it in some of his later stories where he presents fine but mistaken characters in whom "the capacity merely to receive love would already by itself be a sufficient sign of the renunciation of false gods—the missions, ambitions, scruples and decorums—they have been pursuing to their ruin, and therefore the first sign also of their recognition of and submission to the law of love."[10]

It is more difficult to receive love than to give it whenever people have been through experiences that have stifled them yet made them feel guilty about wanting to break out of their prison, or forced them to lie low and not risk close engagement with life, or left them nervous about asserting themselves for fear of a hostile response. It may be that all of us both want and fear to be absolutely loved and this is why we shrink somewhat from God's huge love. As Carson McCullers wrote in *The Ballad of the Sad Café*, "The curt truth is that, in a deep, secret way, the state of being beloved is intolerable to many. The beloved fears and hates the lover, and with the best of reasons. For the lover is forever trying to strip bare his beloved. The lover craves any possible relation with the beloved, even if this experience can cause him only pain."

In the realm of bearing, what has to be borne has to be borne now. We never have to bear today what we shall have to bear tomorrow. It is not God's will that we play neurotic games with the future and try to feel now the weight of burdens not yet laid on us. If we knew the future, how dark it may be, we might lose heart. If we knew the future, how bright it is, we might relax that tension in our concern about our present duty that means we put our utmost into it. So God's will for us concerns what he wants us to do in the present. All he asks us to bear is only for now, and he offers sufficient power for this assignment. If we add to it the thought of tomorrow's evil we shall fall.

There is, however, a certain thinking about the future which is part of today's duty. It is not worthwhile yielding today to impulses that entail conduct we shall be ashamed of tomorrow or regard as unnecessarily timid then. Maturity involves a sane estimate of the results of action and the probable turn of events. It is part of Christian experience that what seems beforehand unbearable is usually found to be bearable when it comes if we are willing to receive all the grace that is available. The requirement is an ongoing readiness to be strengthened to meet what comes, to receive, as Jesus put it, what will be given us in that hour. This readiness and openness to experience is the bloom of the fruitful all-weather faith that Christ gave his church. De Caussade was once advising a nun who had complained that she could not sustain the demands of her life. He advised her to explain the situation to her Superior (who could, of course, have been a woman of mediocre insight), to accept what she decided, and then offer to God

> your dislikes, your health, and even your life, never doubting that God, who has never been known to forsake those who abandon themselves to him, will inspire her who is charged to manifest to you his will to tell you what is necessary. One of three things will infallibly happen: either you will be relieved of your office, or God will sustain and preserve you in it, or else he will allow you to succumb and will take you to himself out of this wretched life.... Whatever happens, then, keep firm after making your attempt. Live or die in peace. We will not speak about it any more, it is God's affair, and no longer yours. He well knows how to make everything turn to your advantage and to his own greater glory.

Chapter 10

THE CRUCIFIXION

All of us find life manageable only if we can impose some order on the rapid flow of experience. We interpret what happens to us and come to a sense of control as we recognize the familiar, relate the new to the known, lessen the impact of what seems dangerous. This continual process of interpretation and arrangement either makes life increasingly interesting and more life available to us or it insulates us from experience and limits what we shall see and understand according to our personal needs. Actually we all continually need both to have our experience enlarged and also to be defended from what we cannot take just now. Whether the mental house we live in has more windows than shutters, or more shutters than windows, death kicks down the door and lets the elements in. By the death of someone they love, or just the thought of death to someone at ease in his possessions, human beings are made aware of their situation as moving towards dying.

Christians have traditionally made the contemplation of death part of their prayer. The death of Christ both deeply perturbed and eventually put courage into the first believers and associated all their hope about human life with a certain kind of dying. Death itself is what everything and everyone comes to as far as we can see, so that we cannot understand life without a view of death. If we attempt to live without giving some meaning to death, if only a provisional one, we are obliged to live awkwardly, involved unconsciously in nervous attempts to cover up our finitude.

The Christian view of death establishes itself in the minds of Christians as they live by the meaning Jesus gave to life. It is not that they first "solve" the problem of death and therefore find life worth living. They find life worth living in Christ and from within that joy see death in a new and exciting light.

Christians in every generation, learning Jesus' way of understanding life, have made time for looking at the cross, as in other religions believers make use of linear symbols or mandalas representing the nature of God or reality, as an aid to contemplation. The cross is used in Christian prayer as an extremely concise emblem of infinite meaning, a summarizing image of the whole Christ event. Its power lies in its carrying so much of what Christians think about God, man, life, and love, not because it isolates, awfully, the moment of Christ's death as in itself making a difference to their relationship to God. Even so, it cannot completely express the Christian idea. What any religion is about is never found in one place but dispersed throughout its ceremonial, its theology, the diverse meanings of its pictorial and literary iconography, and the imageless silence in which the deepest religious saying and loving ultimately come to rest.

We cannot hold all this in the mind at once. We must break it up into portions that we can at least begin to grasp. Some facts of life are only seen clearly if periodically they are seen by themselves, without the other features of experience that qualify them and soften the shock of their impact in the mind. Death is the most bewildering of these facts. The Christian is all the time learning how to say God and death in one breath, in the same sentence.

He can do it in the light of the resurrection, but he must not let the light of the resurrection abolish the darkness of death too easily. Christian prayer slows down every year in passiontide because to move too quickly to the joy of Easter produces a facile and superficial religion of answers to human problems. Pascal said that Christ will be in agony to the end of the world. The Christian life in time is more a grappling with life's wrongness and contradictions by the help of God than a satisfaction over answered problems. The eloquent preaching of Christ as the great answer to all the world's problems lessens the credibility of Christianity and makes thinking people suspect that religion is a form of the superficiality of life.

In the realism of Christian prayer believers put themselves alongside the woman who watches her son dying and sees all she most deeply loves swept away by life's outrageous evil. Jesus, *in extremis*, called her "woman" rather than "mother." She has certainly come to stand for more than a certain mother in a single history of love, she has gathered archetypal feminine significance as girl, daughter, bride, mother through whom half of the meaning of life uniquely flows. She is at once the first ever to be shaken by the mystery of Jesus, and the original believer led into the great temptation to think that what she believes in is finished, so that the church sees itself in her and prays intensely for faith.

As Christians have tried to understand what it was that the mother of Jesus was looking at when she stood at the foot of the cross, they have come to think that far from it being a man abandoned by God it was in fact God himself, so much in the raging sea of truth and half-truth and fear and intrigue and defeated love in which much of human life is lived that he is overwhelmed. Critical minds may well ask what it means to speak of God as carried under in the tragedy of life, but the Christian believes the truth to be something like that. Today much traditional religious assurance fails to convince us. The demonstrable God of old style philosophers and theologians is dead. So is the god we use to explain everything or to make people behave or help them behave, and the god we are sure will keep the church alive, prevent a third world war, and somehow make up to us in some radiant beyond our sad losses here. All that Christians have is God in the center of life, identified with man in Christ, drowning in the cruel sea of death and failure, revealing himself obscurely, ambiguously, so that we have to ask interminably what it all means and whether anything we say about him makes sense. At the cross he seems to be completely surrendered to man's freedom and destroyed by an angry and hateful world. But Christians see a deeper surrender there which gives an incalculable weight of meaning to the cross. It is not difficult to believe in the presence of God in those places and events where life is conspicuously beautiful and happy. Christian faith, without denying or even doubting what is given us then, is deeply committed to the conviction that the kingdom of God comes, comes with power, in the kind of situation in which a man asks why he has been forsaken but does not himself abandon God.

We cannot complain to God for making us creatures that die. Since death comes to everyone it must be part of God's providence. Untimely death and death associated with the evil of life are major forms of suffering and naturally arouse question and revolt, but in itself the fact that we die is an aspect of God's love. We begin to see how this can be as we realize that in a temporal world death is necessary if life is to have a meaning. To go on living forever in time would be meaningless. Meaning cannot be found in endless time, it can only be given in eternity. Eternity is the dimension of meaning for the Christian, the dimension indicated by the words "the kingdom of God."

The idea of the self leads to a similar conclusion. A sense of being a self is possible only in a world of limits. We cannot understand what an undying self could be, except that it would not be able to register value, it would never be stirred by importance and urgency.

Death and time seem to belong together as the conditions under which human beings can learn faith and love. Death helps us to see what is worth trusting and loving and what is a waste of time. If I were to die tomorrow, have I had joy? Have I cared? Have I had the best of what was available? Have I had any of what it is all for?

This situation seems to be practically the same for unbelievers as for believers. Those who think in terms of a future life of increased opportunities to learn and practice faith and love want to come to death as people who have made some progress in the life of trust and affection because that kind of life is going to occupy them more deeply and interestingly after death. Those who think that their dying is simply the bursting of one more meaningless bubble of self-conscious life know that that belief does not invalidate the wisdom of seeking the richest and deepest experience possible in this world, though they must see such experience in a sadder light as the years before them diminish.

Life can be worth the energy it takes to live it only if it is governed by something that is stronger than death, by the decision for acts and enjoyments that imply a contempt of death, a protest against it, indeed a denial of its power to ruin our human day. If the future is death, if life is ultimately for death and this thought prevails in our life, we can hardly live at all.

Life is made possible, because meaningful, by those things we would go on with if we knew death was coming next week. The only things that qualify for this august accolade are those that are not made to look absurd by the thought of death but rather make death look absurd, make it difficult to believe that life is all for death.

Certainly the fuller and richer people's experience of life is, the less death seems to matter to them, as though it might be true that perfect love of life must necessarily cast out the fear of death. Henry James said of a future life that it "isn't really a question of belief... it is on the other hand a question of desire, but of desire so confirmed as to leave belief a comparatively irrelevant affair."[11]

Whether death or God is the future, life is made livable by defiance of death. There are some brave expressions of this defiance. Baudelaire said that even if God did not exist religion would still be holy. A Jesuit priest, Fr. Auguste Valensin, wrote: "If the inconceivable should happen and on my deathbed it should be proved to me incontrovertibly that I am wrong, that there is no life after death, that indeed there is no God, I would have no regrets about believing in him. I would consider that it was to my credit that I believed in him and that if the universe is so ridiculous and contemptible it is just too bad for it. The mistake was not in me for having thought that God exists but in God for not existing."

The only death to be feared, in Jesus' view, is spiritual death, the death of the heart that can no longer want or cheer or protest because it is overcome by indifference or despair. It is not true that death is the last enemy, if it is the death of the body that is in mind. The last enemy to be conquered is hell. It is spiritual death. The name is not important; the essence of it is separation from God, whether this side or the other side of death.

This is why love and concern for those who have died has such an important place in Christian spirituality. A religion of love must remember the dead. There are so many of them and they have done so much for us. Recognition of this fact is expressed in thankfulness and the desire to commemorate. Human love is normally a feeble light. It brightens only the area of our immediate experience. If more love was available to us it would bring past and future into view. The dead and the unborn would become our concern.

In Christianity this civilized sensitiveness to the continuity of life is deepened as believers become aware of the characteristic element in which their Christian life is lived, the surrounding fellowship of all who share and

have shared the church's thankfulness for Christ and conviction of his presence. For them the dividing categories of
near and far, living and dead, are all transcended in the
intense now of Christian prayer.

This kind of love prays as naturally for the dead as for
the living. Some of the energy we misuse in the excessive
regard we have for the Christian past in the form of its traditions, buildings, and institutions would be better
employed in love for the people of the past who are one
with us in Christ. We believe them to be still learning
what we are learning, what love is and does, and with all
the possibilities of progress and failure and the need of
helps which learning implies.

It then becomes a natural thing to pray that they may
have grace to do God's will as it is signified to them there
where they are. We offer ourselves to God so that our love
and life may have some place in his blessing of them if he
so wills, just as we desire to have some part in God's aid to
people in this life for whom we intercede.

The living and the dead may need each other as the
two sides of a coin need each other but we cannot know
how much because of the limitations of our existence in
space and time. From their side the dead may similarly not
forget us as they fulfill their discovered range of God's purpose. If they are still the people we knew, they will not
want to stop loving us. Their hope will be that their
progress in response to God will have some place in his
drawing us to himself.

We believe that God has blessing to give us in response
to our prayers for one another because such prayers, when
in Christ's name, are forms of the love he wishes us all to
learn in increasing depth. The communion of saints can
then be conceived as a continual interplay of giving and
receiving and thanking and giving in gratefulness and joy,
but the mind cannot grasp such a realm of limitless mutuality. We need representative figures to summarize and
symbolize the vaster thing. The special form and instance

of the intercession of the church triumphant is the Blessed Virgin Mary. So we pray, believing that she stands for and in an infinite world of love, "pray for us, holy Mother of God, that we may be made worthy of the promises of Christ."

The cross has its central place in the Christian imagination not because it brings to a focus Christian thoughts about death (though it does this incidentally) but because it is the place of the death of Jesus. When a man's death is directly due to his beliefs and the way of life they entail, particularly when he is aware for a long time that things must so grimly turn out for him but need not if only he will change, his whole life stands before us in a uniquely clear light. Even so, we may not be disposed to give any unique authority to what he said and did and stood for. We shall, however, look at it particularly intently, because not many people die this way. Most people die by accident or disease.

When people look intently at what Jesus said and did it seems to some of them that they are standing in as bright a light as ever shone on our human affairs. They come to the decision that this is going to be for them the truth about life; they are drawn into the community of those who regard Jesus as the truth, and they begin exploring its meaning there.

It becomes clear to them that Jesus set himself to bring men the liberating truth about the human condition and that it was this that cost him his life. Anyone who has no more than begun to know the relaxation of anxiety and the new interest in life that come from understanding it in Jesus' way can see how this makes him one of the infinite number of people for whom Jesus lived and died. He sees now that the essential and normative Christian prayer must be a thanksgiving for Jesus.

The principal sign of growth in the spiritual life is the spread of this thankfulness. As more features of our life take on a new look as matters for gratitude, particularly parts of our experience which we have consistently resented, we begin to realize how it is possible to say, as we do in the Eucharist, that there can be no time or place, however horrible, in which thankfulness would not be the right state of mind.

It is a help to think of the life and death of Jesus as sacrifice, but the word needs to be used with care. In the world of religion a sacrifice is either an offering to the ultimately holy or the giving up of something in devotion to the holy. The two ideas can blend in a single instance but it is wise to keep them apart because the first meaning is infinitely important, the second infinitely dangerous. To give is at once expressive and liberating. To give up suggests reluctance; it implies that one needs or is perhaps particularly identified by this thing which is to be surrendered for some laudable reason. There was nothing about Jesus that he wanted to keep. He found his identity in giving.

People who do not want to give think it is more blessed to give than to receive because giving is painful. There are others who actually sense the enjoyment of existence through giving, through spending and being spent. For these it is more blessed to give than to receive not because there is virtue in it but because there is happiness in it.

Jesus was this kind of giver. He is the great sign to us that life need not be dreary, need not be saved, but can be, must be, entirely spent. It is fear that makes us hold on to life or to what represents life's meaning for us. The cross marks the place in history where a superb victory over fear was won, the public fear in religion and politics, the private fear within the individual's insecurities. The proof of that is simply the verdict of time, that at the cross it is clear that life is represented by the man who died there and death by the people who put him there.

And he is still with us, after all these years, still making a huge difference to the life of the world. The situation that faces human beings has not changed from his day to ours. It never changes. We are always involved in the struggle with dishonesty and pretension, tempted to premature despair, likely to be frightened of truth and love, wanting the real but often making do with the substitute. To this persisting human situation no one has ever spoken so relevantly as Jesus and provided such hopeful and productive comment on it. To take stock of the politicians, trade union officials, and other opinion-formers whose pronouncements the mass media shove into our mind is to find oneself longing for this one Son of Man whose mind looms over our confusion with its unfading clarity, its startling bite on reality. It is a relief to be in his presence, not because he has the answers but precisely because he inhabits a world of meaning in which it is worthwhile asking questions.

More than any other he was a man exposed to the joy and humiliation of experience, born to love and to suffer, to articulate the deepest longings of human beings and make clear what there is in reality to correspond with them. He saw life as haunted by an extraordinary urgency, as though heaven is always just down the road from you; just a few steps and you would be there, sobbing with joy in the great forgiveness. Yet he saw the mistaken choices people make in the urgency of their longing for joy and he tried to persuade them to relax the tension of that search and have only one care, to want and trust God. It seems a vague prescription at first but it has the power to discharge our situations of egoism and fear, and a whole world of grace is waiting to pour into the space left by them. But we are complicated creatures in whom realistic desires struggle continually with attitudes that once worked but do not any longer, and we cannot acquire the mind of Jesus overnight. We have to learn how to make wanting and trusting God our one care, to learn what Jesus meant by "God" and distinguish it from what we would like that august word to mean, and we shall often get it all wrong. We need all the help there is.

Chapter 11

THE
RESURRECTION

She had all along believed that she and her son were involved in some extraordinary fate. She had lived in a continual waiting for the thing to happen about him that was to happen, in which it would all become clear. She was a woman of silences. In these she had often tried to put together the clues dropped at intervals into her mind, from the mysterious beginning of her motherhood to the last humiliation through which life had dragged her. She could hardly take any more of existence and began to doubt all she had thought about him, all he had said to her, but she came to no conclusions. She remained the woman of silences, exhausted but still waiting for the light in which she would see the signs coming together into a meaning.

She was not alone. She was the still center of the group that had formed round him and was being brought closer together by the memory of all that he was, now that all that he was was memory.

When we reach the end there is no going back. We can never by some magical cancellation of all that we have gone through be as we were. All we can do is press further and deeper into this "end," experiencing it more, making sure that it is the end of whatever is truly over and that we have accepted the end of what cannot come again. By such acceptance we win a release from the nostalgias and resentments that fasten the mind obsessionally in the past. We become emotionally free to examine this end, this loss—and to discover that it is not absolute.

It is not the case that everything has ended. Life has not ended, nor the network of relationships that human life is. This grief is loss not only for us privately but for others too. If we had the imagination we would see it as infinite in its effects, involving the whole, of which we so painfully feel our part, and indeed God himself whose is the earth and the fullness of it and the emptiness of it, whose will it is that we should know what is to be done now.

To this group, remembering their tragic Jesus, waiting for the future, wanting to know if this pain is all, if they are meant for nothing more than to see what they love die and what they believe in defeated, ready for this if it be the case, the experience of resurrection comes.

People say that they have seen him. What has happened to them is so like his presence as they remember it that it must be his return. They are all, of course, people who have been close friends of Jesus. No one else but they could possibly recognize any experience as his presence. Only people who had known and loved him could say what "seeing him" means.

The Christian is always in the Easter situation of the first friends of Jesus, either discovering the presence of Christ for himself or knowing that some of his friends are doing this and longing to learn how to interpret his own experience in terms of such assurance and joy.

It is within the group he must learn this. The presence of Christ, the risen Christ (because no one doubts that he has died) is known only in the Christian community. In his oneness with God he certainly appears to millions of others in other forms, to which they give strange names drawn from the vocabulary of their own spiritual tradition, but it is only in the Christian church that he can be known as the risen Christ, because it is only there that such words have any meaning.

It is not possible to convince a Jew, a Hindu, a Buddhist, an atheist that Christ has risen. But if someone comes into the life of the Christian community and learns its way of thinking, praying, and acting, he may come to the conclusion that the language we use about our experiences is reasonable; for example, he may come to see that it makes sense to say that what happens at the Eucharist is the presence of Christ.

People believe in the resurrection of Jesus because they are in the church. No one else does. The first generation of those who saw in Jesus the meaning of life and committed themselves to his deep satisfaction and hopes discovered with astonishment that his death made no difference to their vision of his importance or their commitment to all he stood for, all he was. They learned that what they remembered as him was with them again, especially in the intensity of their experience at the Eucharist.

Not everything that happened in the experience of the early church was "the Lord." He had to be identified. He still has to be identified. In the life of faith there will always be an alternatively excited and dubious asking where he is, whether this could possibly be the Christ, how that can be understood as the healing presence when it hurts so much, and again and again the conviction that that indeed was he and I did not want to know him, or he called me then and I did what I thought I could by way of response, and he blessed me there.

As people learn the church's language, become familiar with its idea of love and its hopes about the end, and share its continual sense of being under the judgment as well as under the smile of Christ, its inward groan "while we wait for God to set us wholly free," their skeptical friends may not see anything that relates significantly to the Jesus of the New Testament. All they may indeed see is a group of out-of-date people still acting in their absurd repertory, not realizing that the curtain is down and the theater empty.

But to those who seek Christ within the church things begin to happen. They begin to see a consistency between the characteristically Christian experiences and the meaning the church gives them. They sense the substance prevailing from the beginning until now. They come to believe that in the ambivalence of it all he may be found at any time. It is possible to understand some unhappy meeting in the damp-walled room of a church that must soon close as a resurrection appearance, as the voice of one saying "Reach your fingers here, see my hands." He can also pull at the mind so persistently that you may wish you had never heard of him.

This is not to deny that the God and Father of our Lord Jesus Christ expresses himself outside the church in mercy and reconciliation and human nobility and the pursuit of happiness and truth. The church sees these as works of the Father and the Spirit with whom the Son is one. But there is a unique work of God in Christ in that for us Christ is the source and norm of our understanding of life, he is at the center of all our deepest relief and thanks and praise and fear. It is as those whose view of life and truth is so formed that we greet the Jew, the Hindu, the Buddhist, the scientific humanist and want to make our interested and expectant way into their experience, to learn what they along their different route have found to be thankful for and to love.

St. Luke describes two first-generation Christians coming to conviction about the resurrection. Two men are walking from Jerusalem to a village not far away. It is late in the day. The light is weakening, everything earthly is held in a vesperal suspense while these two friends talk about the contradictions and disappointments of life and the work of Jesus and the way it has all come to nothing. They want to understand. The truth of God in Christ is shown as very near to them, as it must be to all who want the truth so desperately.

As the temporal day declines for them, the truth comes nearer. There is a dawning of a spiritual day. This happens often enough in the inner life of human beings. One of the advantages of maturity is its capacity to entertain a new form of mental life. Youth is normally not yet ready for this, being occupied in establishing itself in other terms.

At the beginning of their walk to Emmaus Jesus is to them simply an ordinary man, as he is for everyone setting out on the journey of faith. They only see him for what he really is through a kind of release in the mind which makes possible a deeper understanding of life and Jesus' place in life.

This release takes time to complete its effect. There is an awareness of a presence, though who or what it is is not clear. There is the examination of the past in the light of the traditional wisdom in which they have grown up. There are Jesus' own words about himself and his relationship with his people's historic struggles and hopes. As these matters come together more clearly in their minds the two friends grow fond of this man. They do not merely admire his grasp of things, they want more of his company. This want seems to grow in depth as the night deepens and grows cold and the stars emerge and throw around their meaningless light. There is a meal, graced with ritual. There is a moment of recognition which ends almost as soon as its thrilling passage has lit up their minds, but it leaves them much altered by its transitory excitement, it leaves them people who have reason to believe.

In his other book about the spread of Christianity St. Luke describes the first Christians as keeping together in the teaching, in the fellowship, in the breaking of bread, and in the prayers. It is a situation foreshadowed in this

Emmaus experience. The teaching is Jesus' opening to them the scriptures. The fellowship is their oneness, their hearts burning within them as he talked with them by the way. The prayers are this basic posture of Christian affection and need—"Stay with us," which is a way of saying "Lord, have mercy upon us," or, "The grace of our Lord Jesus Christ be with us all." The breaking of the bread is explicitly there.

Intuition grows into faith as we make our journey within the life of the church. Christian faith is not something you prove first and then practice. It has been said that you cannot have it by a sort of mental hire purchase system by which you get it all before you have paid for a quarter of it. It comes, it grows, as you take your place responsibly within the fellowship, the teaching, the prayer, the sacramental life, and the pain and perplexity of the church of Christ.

This is not to say that there is any easy way to faith in the risen Christ. All of the disciples came to their individual moment of recognition after much perplexity. And when they knew him it was not a mere recognition that it was Jesus, it was that perception in depth that activated their memory, the hints left in the mind as they had struggled all the way through to understand life, and all the hope and love that had been gathering round the image of Jesus. The cumulative result of all this was that at last they saw him as the Lord.

The presence of Christ in the church does not prove our own resurrection. It is part of our faith that it shows the possibility of resurrection, and indeed that it is representative of God's will to raise every man to a new dimension of life. But Jesus was a unique being who knew how to live. All he had to live and love with was continually available to him and continually used. He saw no need to keep anything of his marvelous self in reserve for some more important or more taxing moment than the present. It is not difficult to agree with Peter that "it could not be that death should keep him in its grip." But there is nothing about our dingy performance that suggests the rightness of its being raised from death.

We believe in the resurrection of the dead because it is part of the teaching of Jesus as well as woven into his life. It would also seem in itself unbelievable that if God has a purpose for men and women and this purpose is the expression of his love it should culminate in their destruction. Reasonableness returns to the human scene and credibility to God only if death is a stage in men's continuing experience of understanding and response to that purpose until it is realized in an end that all will see is consistent with fatherly love.

However, none of that kind of reasoning forms the *characteristic* Christian comment on this dark subject, which if we give it more than a moment's attention brings us all up against our loneliness.

The authentic Christian experience is that of entering into a new freedom from anxiety and self-preoccupation, a new happiness and tranquility in discovering the worth and wisdom of loving. It is an experience within the fellowship of the church, and from the very beginning it was interpreted as the presence of Jesus because all that was precisely the kind of thing he so intensely was.

Christians have understood their characteristic experience in this way ever since. They believe that Christ is indeed their deep inner life. He is the one of whom the church's holy writings speak; he is the real presence in its sacraments; he is the thankfulness and love that in spite of sin bind together its members in the fellowship of the Spirit, though its unity still waits the clear demonstration we all long for; he is the one who raises a cheerful flame in the mind's smoking flax of faith.

It is within this intense experience of memory and desire that the church repeatedly finds a voice in such classical prayers and assurances as "Thou, O Lord, art in the midst of us and we are called by thy name. Leave us not, we beseech thee," and "Whether we live we live unto the Lord and whether we die we die unto the Lord. Whether we live therefore or die, we are the Lord's." If we are his and he is in the midst of us, he whose power and most vulnerable presence death tried and utterly failed to stop, the agonizing problem of our last day is over now, and from henceforth blessed are the dead who die in the Lord.

Even so we are not yet at the center of what Christ has done to death. He has not merely taken the fear out of it. It is believed that in the presence of Christ there is a fantastic overlapping of time and eternity and in that glorious confusion of dimensions death seems almost to have disappeared, has to be looked for. Heaven, the fulfillment of God's purpose, is understood in terms of the presence of Christ; accordingly, those who have Christ so really, even if still incompletely, now, cannot help feeling that death has been bypassed. They have already in a sense passed to that further life. At any rate the glory of that intenser union to come sheds an anticipatory light on their affairs, as sometimes emerging from sleep we sense even among the absurdities and terrors of a dream the saner light of the arriving day.

As a problem to think through (though as a moment to die through it still waits in its hidden hour) death can be settled in advance for the believer, by faith, by his being the Lord's, being in Christ. People who live intensely for Christ's idea of love and his delight in existence know in their moments of reflection that life is this and this life and this is all you need to know. All life's voices are growing more interesting and meaning more, and you begin to see something in Jesus' idea that he and his friends, not very wise, not very wealthy, not very secure, were enjoying now what past ages with all their legendary illustrious, their prophets and kings, desired and waited for but were denied.

It can never be like that always, for anyone, and for some it must rarely be so. Some people's lives are made of such suffering and injustice that they are hardly worth the effort it takes to negotiate each twenty-four hours; or they are so deteriorated with age and weakness that they long to be finished with what seems such a useless assignment. When such longing is lifted up to God we do not believe that the arms of mercy in which we are all obscurely held loosen their hold on us in the slightest. But our freedom to do some part of the will of God is never taken from us. Even if all that can be offered to God is the rejection of a sterile or self-pitying acceptance of the evil situation and some attempt at courage and hope and waiting on God, a shaft of the eternal light makes a patch of heaven there. God cannot want from us what is not possible. When we are as personalities so reduced that we cannot entertain the thoughts and intentions of faith and love, God no longer wants his will done by us, he wants it done for us by others.

All human beings live and grow through various forms of dying. Anyone who wants to find life worth living, its interest surviving its boredom, must be ready for death. Beethoven said it was a poor sort of man who did not know how to die. He said he had known how to die since he was in his teens. Certainly death is making inroads into the substance of our life from that age. But Beethoven, and many others with his knowledge of what life is, was not interested in the waning power of this or that part of our physical constitution. He was interested in the nature of experience.

Every new experience alters us; if it is important it breaks us open, may even make a new being of us. We lose something that once meant life to us. Something in us dies, even if it is just a way of thinking that no longer protects us or helps us to manage experience without distress. Something new comes to life in us, even if it is only an interest in living authentically, in being oneself instead of an echo of one's parents or one's church or one's social group.

When this personal transformation ceases we are finished, we are dead souls. Many people's lives come to an end long before they die. It is a fate that threatens us all. The organ to be watched is not the heart, the anatomical heart, whose failure gives you clinical death. What needs to be watched is the spiritual heart, the heart with which we love, which Jesus said we can and should use wholly, recklessly, in loving God and man, whose failure means you have exhausted your possibilities. When that happens and there is nothing left remarkable beneath the visiting moon, your sound anatomical heart is no use at all to you, except to be traded in for one crowded hour.

Christianity is a religion of new life through death. The death and resurrection of Christ are meaningless unless they are events in our own lives today. It does not matter to me if I am told that someone got through death somehow some two thousand years ago and appeared in some form, still awaiting proof, unless in my own life now there is some analogue of such a fantastic process. But we believe that nothing was made without him, which means that every human life, to make the most of its possibilities, must follow the pattern of his life and go through his process of dying to live.

It is certain that the most inert and deadly people are those who have never known the death of love, or faith, or hope. The people who give the impression of being vital and interesting and make living worthwhile are people who have seen one or other of the many faces of death and believed it still possible to begin again, worthwhile trying again.

The risen Christ is the wounded Christ, not the transfigured one. This part of the resurrection language carries the church's faith that the one they recognized that Sunday at Emmaus, and the one they heard saying "this is my body" that Thursday in the upper room, is one and the same as the one who has been loved, lived for, known in the breaking of the bread, and died for all the way through, and the one we shall all ultimately see face to face and recognize as the love within all our loves.

Since he is that one presence of God, his wounds take on a new meaning. From being signs that he bears on his body the marks of man's hatred they become symbols of God's love, to be read as saying that the love who nevertheless suffers and the sufferer who nevertheless continues to love are not merely descriptions of the man Jesus but disclosures of what God is and what he gives when he gives himself. This means that if, when you have received him (say, in the Eucharist), it is asked what in fact you have that you did not have before you knelt at that place "where prayer has been valid" so long, the answer is that you have now in you the grace to love and to know that it is worth its cost, and you have the power to receive pain and not be turned against life by it; but all this is a kind of bare potential as yet, a something waiting to be used in encounter with the first lovable or hateable thing or person you next meet.

Christian comment on the good life uses to the full the image of dying-to-live, and naturally, because it is an idea with a marvelously extended relevance. But there is a limit to the meanings that can be extracted from it.

The new life in Christ, upon which we enter by baptism and conversion, the risen life as it is sometimes called, is not absolutely new. It is a commonplace in Christian experience that converts frequently overstate this newness, exaggerating both their pre-conversion sin and their post-conversion change for the better. There is no such thing as a completely new life. A newborn baby is not a completely new physical event; the convert, born again, is not an entirely new spiritual life. This is because existence is a moving flux, not a series of unconnected events; it is a continuum in which memory and therefore learning are possible and traces and scars are necessarily left.

We may often want to grasp the sorry scheme of things and remold it nearer to the heart's desire, and it is normal to want this and occasionally to dream at length about it. It is part of romanticism to build an attitude on it. It is part of neuroticism to long seriously for it, for some completely new world where we shall begin again the brave experiment of life without memories, without persisting resentments and compensatory longings, without any form of hangover from yesterday.

If a Christian longs for a completely new life, without rational or moral connections with this life, he is really detaching the dream of paradise from the faith in which such a dream is valid and credible. He is wanting to escape from continuity. In the secret depths of that want lies the death-wish, not the longing for eternal life.

The Christian dream of paradise is a necessary part of a structure of meaning in which human beings are seen as lovers and seekers whose loving and seeking demand a larger context than time for their completion.

Time and eternity, this life and what comes after it, form a whole. They are the facts, they are all that is, they are reality. You cannot extract yourself or escape or abscond. There is nowhere else to go. The continuity of things does not seem to be broken ever, though it is a continuity of growth and change.

To meditate the resurrection means thinking of one in whom this continuity is made clear to us. He carries scars and recognizable grace from the realm of time and he bears also anticipatory indications of the realm beyond time. We are to understand that the two realms belong together. Their interrelatedness makes the interest and meaning of our life.

Through our response to God in Christ Jesus and through letting it mold and inform our delight in people and things we learn what it means to love. To long for paradise is to approve of life as so understood, as a learning of love however long it takes, and to believe that we shall eventually learn it.

That skill, that heaven, will not be given to us at death because that would contradict the moral structure of reality. There cannot be any prize just for dying.

Dying is not worth anything. Death is not anything one does. It is a matter of having earthly life taken from us. Certainly this happens infinitely variously; for example, naturally, in extreme old age and sometimes beautifully then, sometimes unexpectedly without time to think or speak before thought and speech are drowned, or resentfully as though it means a possession torn from reluctant fingers, or horribly in calamity or war, or nobly and with full awareness in religious and political martyrdoms where it is a thing magnificently chosen to be suffered and so an act of vast moral worth.

The circumstances of dying may or may not give opportunity for the expression of our loving, but dying itself must be our introduction to opportunities of further learning, more sensitive loving, deeper transforming of our self-preoccupation into loving. It cannot give us the ultimate, it cannot open to us the gate of heaven. Our learning about love, and its joy and trust, must necessarily be incomplete at our death, to be completed elsewhere.

To meditate the resurrection, and the risen Christ himself in whom time and beyond-time meet, is to consider some of these facts of faith. It is also to see that the dead in Christ are still our friends, still of our company in the search for truth and the learning of love. Friendship here cannot be without correspondence with friendship beyond. They must need our love and prayers, and it is a relief to know that we can happily give this depth of ourselves to them. And they will surely give us their love and prayers, as God makes this (for us so needed) thing possible to them.

The idea of dying to live has had a long history and in the world of imagery is itself a world of inexhaustible interest but it does not come so naturally to our minds now. The change which a person of our time experiences through the adoption of Christian attitudes and aims does not call, at any rate in its early stages, for such dramatic and absolute terms to describe it. Sudden conversions that wring the amazed and agitated believer with the spiritual shudders are not part of our religious news. People want to take their time, must think it all out or at least have a shot at thinking; certainly they suspect the skillful evangelist's power. The debasement of communication achieved by years of political propaganda and commercial advertisement has made us all very cagey, hypersensitive to being in any way manipulated, cynical about every kind of big sell. So, when we speak of what Christ means to us, we want to speak of what we know and as we know it, rejecting histrionic or romantic inflations, uneasy indeed with what used to be called the language of Zion.

If we are to use the dying to live image we do not refer to any absolute transformation that commitment to Christ has brought or is bringing us but simply to the fact that the life of faith is an affair of growth and continual change. Some of the ways in which we have been conducting our relationships and coping with our anxieties no longer serve us, look as if they are in fact hindering us, as we see our true life now in the figure of Christ. We have a glimpse of the new attitudes we will need to adopt, if only we dare risk them, to further the development of this true life. This change in us is slow but we believe it to be deep. It proceeds through hesitations, failures, pains, small encouragements, occasional tranquil intervals in which life feels to have a fresh breeze blowing through it. There comes a stage of conviction that there is now no going back to that old life of ours before the momentous shadow of the approaching Christ had fallen across it. We sense the beginning of a freedom, the start of a new loving, that as they intensify may well make that life seem like death, and perhaps we shall use that great language then.

What we know now is a beginning. There is work to do. Our self is formed and pretty rigid now. The result is that I see the need to change but for the life of me cannot somehow get round to changing.

Many of the attitudes I must alter have themselves been developed as defenses against anxiety. The prospect of not having them to rely on brings into awareness the resentments that underlie them. If I am going to do without continual finding fault with others and with life I may very well begin to see how much I disapprove of myself and the deal I think I have had from God.

The more defensiveness there is in one's life the harder it is to change to spontaneity and love. This is another way of saying that the older one is the harder it is to die to the old self that so inefficiently has carried one so far and to live in the newness one sees in increasingly desirable terms. In the second half of life we progress largely by understanding ourselves and our limitations. This is not in any way a *faute de mieux*. To recognize one's fears, compulsions, and resentments is part of the progress of one's being, it has a loosening effect, it objectifies these aspects of one's life so that one is not immersed in them, one is able to stand at a certain distance from them, even be amused at them.

At the same time it is part of the experience of later life that there are chances of renewal then that do not come earlier. Human beings have not much time for religion in the first third of their life. There is so much concentrated living and deciding to get through in this period that while young people may not be wise in ignoring the depths of life they can reasonably plead some excuse for their preoccupation with other matters. In the middle years the rush of experience begins to lessen. Confrontation with the depths becomes possible and natural. Finding a new orientation of the self is a matter of life and death then in the sense that people must attend to the question what it is all for and what they are for or else run the risk of retreating into a shrinking existence of nostalgias and compensations.

Certainly most Christians in the middle years find the religious ground shaky under their feet. They may have presenting problems of a different kind, domestic issues or elusive personal glooms that resist examination. But underneath, as likely as not, is the Nicodemus situation, the man in his middle years needing to revalue his values, dogged by the question what life is going to mean or can be made to mean from now on and finding most of the interpretation of Christianity with which he has been brought up no longer believable.

The thinking has often to be done all over again, but it is harder now than it was in youth, and in an odd way it has a note of danger in it because the existential anxieties that youth can never feel are nearer the surface of the mind. These are not problems that can be answered, they are mysteries to be lived with and lived through. That kind of living is what faith is for.

The fact is that now is the time and opportunity to learn much more deeply what it means to live by faith. In earlier years so much of one's life is kept going by the sheer momentum of existence, shored up by success, stimulated by the unabating flow of new interests, that usually far less of the goodness of life is due to conscious faith than one imagines. The life of the later years provides faith with room to grow and show itself. It grows by depth rather than extension. The mature Christian normally seems to live deeply by a little, not by a comprehensive system that furnishes bright comment on all the questions. It is one of the special services of old age to faith to make clear how little will do as long as it holds.

This is not to close down on the life of the mind. Anyone who wants a faith that has no place for conscious reflection about its insights and does not attempt to give a

rational account of itself would be far better off with Zen
Buddhism than Christianity, which has always been char-
acterized by a high degree of intellectual activity. The only
thinking Christians need to fear is the kind that is remote
from life or takes one away from life because such thinking is at the expense of loving. The risen Christ says to
Thomas, "Reach your finger here; see my hands. Reach
your hand here and put it into my side." Some people
cringe at such extremely physical symbolism but it may be
that the meaning cannot come home to us in any other
way—that our doubts will destroy our faith unless we are
in close touch with the wounds of the Son of Man, unless
we connect the thinking mind with the suffering world.
The real darkness is not the perplexity of the reason but
the insensitiveness of the affections that does not *feel* the
injuries and insults heaped on the body of humanity in all
the places where life bleeds and hurts.

Chapter 12

THE ASCENSION

A nyone who reads the life of Jesus for the first time must find it tantalizingly mysterious at certain points, particularly at its beginning and at its ending. Compared with the account of Jesus' teaching, or of his last tragic week, the nativity stories and the description of the ascension seem to belong to a world of their own, a world in which there is the appearance of angels (incandescent gentlemen with plumage between the shoulderblades) and other surprises.

They do in fact belong to a special world of speech. It is not the same as, for example, the world of St. Luke chapter 15, in which Jesus speaks so affectingly of a lost coin, a lost animal, a lost son, the truth steadily gathering significance throughout the chapter until it comes to rest in the depths of our minds with the immense final solace of "was lost and is found." It seems to be one voice speaking there, a voice we long to trust.

The nativity and ascension stories belong to another world of speech in that a collective, more elusive voice is saying them, the voice of the young Christian community compelled to draw on the only god-language it knew to express its convictions about Jesus. It is a language of religious gratitude and joy and awe in which the historical and the poetical are inextricably mingled. No other language would do when Christians thought about Jesus' coming into human being and when they made their final assessment of his place in the scheme of things.

So the ascension is not a historical event. It is a way of saying, in the language of a particular religious tradition, that when the deepest questions about God and man, life and death, are being asked, Christians answer them in terms of what they believe about Jesus. That Christians should give Jesus this authority was not merely a matter of decision on their part; it represented something that happened to them, compelling them to make this response to their experience.

As the disciples were looking on, "he was lifted up and a cloud took him out of their sight." The cloud is what it so often is in the Bible, a symbol for the glory of God. As the first generation of Christians "looked on," reflected on the life, death, and resurrection of Jesus, the image of Jesus merged with, was taken up into the glory of God, to become life's meaning set forth and the figure of what God's love is and man's love can be.

It seems that the use of spatial imagery in talk about God is a problem for many people. The idea of God as a *heavenly* father, in some sense *up* somewhere above us, provokes the same irritation and incredulity as does the use in religion of literary forms that are nearer to myth and poetry than they are to history. But religion can no more get along without such means of expression than humanity can live without poetry.

When human beings think of God's majesty, perfection, and creative power, and desire to acknowledge this, the idea of height is much too useful to ignore. Our Christian use of it may well derive from the fact that at an early stage of Old Testament religion God was a mountain-god or sky-god. We belong to a religious tradition that has long been upward-looking and attracted to images of hills, mountains, ascent, and descent in its attempts to become articulate. There is a more fundamental influence in the universal human experience that it is easier to fall than to rise, that to look up to stimulates effort, to look down on brings feelings of satisfaction and a kind of rest. It is natural to describe what we regard as better than us, and worth reaching, as "superior" to us.

When we speak of religion and life in a more self-conscious way, as something happening within our beings, we find a marine symbolism more useful, with its distinction between surface and depth. There are events that do not matter to us very much and those that affect us intensely or more than we realize. To speak about this range of experience would be difficult if we were forbidden to use words like "superficial" and "profound."

Both depth and height language are necessary as long as life comes to us as a deeply felt inward thing and as an appeal of something outside ourselves summoning us to effort and admiration. If we live it by faith it comes to us more in this way than it used to do, and we are glad it does.

The more life expands and reveals its vast dimensions and its mystery, the clearer becomes the need for as many ways of expressing and communicating human experience as possible. Many believers seem reluctant to apply this truth to the Bible. They try to read it as though it is of the same kind of thing as today's issue of *The Times;* they feel guilty if they cannot take as plain history the story of the wise men coming from the east to worship the infant Jesus or the report that the last that was seen of him was his visible levitation into the sky until he became a vanishing speck in the blue.

It is obvious that the church has not successfully made it clear that for centuries it has been the orthodox Christian view that the Bible needs to be interpreted, and that the reader must fairly soon, if he wants to make head or tail of it, see the difference between the religious mean-

ing and the literary form of any given passage. The four-
teenth-century author of *The Cloud of Unknowing* gave
this advice to the Christian world of his day:

> Take care not to interpret physically what is intended
> spiritually, even though material expressions are used,
> like "up, down, out, behind, before, this side, that side."
> The most spiritual thing imaginable, if we are to speak of
> it at all...must always be spoken of in physical words.
> But what of it? Are we therefore to understand it physi-
> cally? Indeed not, but spiritually.

The meaning of the ascension is that the Christian
church believes that Jesus is one with the glory of God and
that his presence in its corporate and individual life is
God's presence. To live by this faith must mean to find life
bathed in the light of an increasing hopefulness and joy.
There cannot be anything better than the presence of
God, now that Jesus has shown us what he is like.
Mankind has had strange notions about the ultimate. It
could be said that we have reason to fear or at any rate dislike God unless someone shows him to us in a better light.
Jesus was entirely given over to God and revealed that
anyone so disposed lives a spontaneous, affectionate, honest, and brave life. Nothing else that we have seen in the
human performance contests our view that Jesus is what a
human being was created to be. We think of Jesus and
God together now, to be trusted and loved, as indeed life
is to be trusted and loved because it is God's love
expressed in time. All this is faith; no one knows it to be
true, no one knows that it is not true.

For years now there has been so much perplexity about
the Christian faith and the church that many of our generation have never allowed themselves or been allowed to
get excited about Jesus of Nazareth, as a holy and mysterious person compelling us to find for our talk about him the
highest categories and best adjectives we know. Only the
great words will do for one who seems to us to understand

life with such penetration and love it so undiscourageably, whose sayings, once they are really heard, do not leave the mind but stay to stir our deepest wants and questions and make us think again of God. Many people, of course, would have had their vision of him long ago if he had not from the beginning been stamped with someone else's uncongenial view of him, sentimental, moralistic, ecclesiastical. It is inevitable in such a personal thing as religion that other people's experience of the Spirit will be either boring or repelling unless they have some gift of self-disclosure or some grace from God that shines through the clumsy utterance. Certainly the Jesus who is little more than an exhortation to the unselfish life and to attention to problems of human freedom in every country in the world except one's own has had a long enough run now and we may reasonably expect his demise shortly. The fact is that faith seems rather more lonely than it used to be; you have to unlearn a lot, ignore aspects of faith that fail to connect with your experience yet, and begin your own search from where you are.

There are others, no doubt, whose experience is totally different, who have always seen him apparelled in celestial light. May he continue for them to be clothed in that radiance from the head down to the feet, secretly building up in them the readiness to trust him in another form when the time comes.

Without some vision of the glorified Christ the life of faith must be more difficult than it need be because it is being lived without its full content of joy. One way out of this impoverishment is provided by the development of closer relations between the churches in recent years. This is producing a mutual enrichment as one tradition learns the way another thinks of Jesus and loves him and doubts him. Particularly it seems that the eastern church has seen the glory of Christ more intensely than the western. In the total response of Christendom to God the west tends to worship God with tears in its eyes because it has so profoundly sensed God's pain, while the east looks up to God with the rapt adoration that is so clearly caught in the faces of an El Greco painting or the serenity of the great icons because it is the glory of God that they have seen and it is that glory they see in Jesus Christ.

Love of the mother of Jesus is a natural outcome of the vision of his glory and also the means of keeping that vision clear, just as giving expresses love and also intensifies it. It has been said that the surest way to avoid the cult of Our Lady is to deny, consciously or unconsciously, the deity of Jesus.

Certainly the element of request or demand in the Christian religion will be infinitely more powerful than the mere appeal of an ideal if we believe that we are not expressing our moral preferences in dramatic terms but are in the presence of God who asks if we can do this for him and his world. And when in the Christian view of life we believe that the infinite demander is also the infinite giver, and that, as St. Augustine said, God gives what he demands, human life becomes an entirely new thing, with possibilities unsuspected by the mind that thinks we have only ourselves to thank or curse for the way things are.

People who have seen the glory of Christ in this way have a religion that is interesting. It is not the case that everyone's religious life is interesting, though people with an intense love of God will rejoice at every sign of his presence. But to see Christ as one with God means that one is summoned by the ultimate. No one turns to God and stays with him forever. The process of turning has to be repeated again and again. Through these repeated returns, confessions, forgivenesses, recommitments, renewals of trust, one grows in the knowledge of God. Only God can call us to this protracted journey. An idea that is just a symbol for our hopes and aspirations will not do it. There is a menacing verse in the New Testament about the man from whom is taken away even what he has. Many people lose their Christian understanding of life. It can happen at any time, in late adolescence, in the middle twenties, in the forties, and with a particularly tragic desolation as they approach the normal end of a human life. They all have tried to live on what they knew of the Christian life. They ceased to see themselves as learners, or they lost this essential vision of Christ as the one who because he is one with God is the infinite claimer because he is the infinite giver.

In the testing situations in which we run out of hope and effort it is a question of what there is "out there" to help us, if there is anything. If it is assumed there is something, we need to know the limits of its power. Is it true that it will never fail us or must we always know that some lonely struggle one day could be the kind of emergency in which its presence is not to be counted on? The Christian faith that Jesus is one with the glory of God has its maximum significance exactly there. In all the hoping, trusting, loving we are learning from Jesus, our working out what it means to abide in him, we are united with the ultimate creative love who is continually working to bring all that exists to fulfillment. He alone knows what our individual fulfillment is. Through our faith in Christ he is at work deep within us to bring it about, and he will never stop doing this, re-ordering our dis-ordered self until, however long it takes, we come to know what it means to love with all that we are.

The learning of love and the unlearning of fear do not ever happen quickly. In the early stages—and most of us for this life at any rate are never further on than the early stages—we are conscious of our incompetence far more than success. It soon becomes clear that whether we go on with the life of faith or not depends on how much hope we have.

It is possible to see how mistakenly one has been managing a given area of life and that there is a better way and yet not have much interest in choosing it. We have not enough hope about ourselves to feed the thought that this particular change could in fact come. The clear sight of the better way simply stirs a listless longing. Sometimes we have so little of this hope that we cannot acknowledge that we have any spiritual problems at all because that would mean looking into the sad eyes of our weakness, so we project our need for reorientation onto our circumstances or our health and gloom about these.

Prayer is both the natural expression of Christian faith and its vitalizer. The adoration of the glorified Christ and the contemplation of his oneness with the Father inevitably arouse hope and joy. It is not the function of adoration to produce joy because, so understood, the multitudinous beauty of Christian praise becomes a mere pattern of incantatory formulae without reference to what is in fact the state of things. The purpose of adoration is to express faith, to say with utmost joy what we believe to be true, that as we open ourselves to Christ we become receptive to that ultimate power and love who is working continually to bring all things to fulfillment and lead all men and women out of their hates and prejudices and grievances into happiness.

But the expression of belief naturally deepens the hold of its truth in our minds; and the meaning of this hold is that we are being held by God because his truth is not an inert idea but his energizing presence. It is only as so held, by one who will be with us whatever heaven or hell we walk, that we can sustain that part of the inner life of faith which is journey into self-understanding.

Any attitude which is the result of a mistaken management of life has a number of needs at its root and these have to be made clear before change is possible. When Christ is admitted into the life of someone who, for example, now becomes aware of his tendency to self-depreciation or to talk excessively about his misfortunes or to choose the unfair and the sad in life for comment rather than the amusing and encouraging, these impoverishing habits are not loosened easily. He may have now to discover how far the resentment which they indicate has penetrated his experience, how his resources of hope have drained away, and for what particular reason he has so long disliked life. It is God's will that we make this kind of self-discovery at the same time as our knowledge of Christ grows and we become more certain of his presence in the sacraments and more fascinated by his image in the New Testament. Self-knowledge without some mercy that makes it productive will simply take us down into the night. The more interested we are in the Christian way, in interpreting life as God speaking to us, the more we can take and use our self-discoveries. They are signs of the life-giving and healing presence who means to release our loving from the fury and fear that stifle it.

The ascension of Christ seems to have been for the first Christians the spiritualization of religion. In the Easter story when Mary rushed forward to embrace Jesus in a turmoil of excited recognition and love there is something odd about him. He who never held anyone at arms' length, who incessantly longed to communicate and share, says, "Touch me not."

We understand this surprising reserve to mean that Christ's presence with his friends was passing from the physical to the spiritual. The norm of Christian experience is not that of the first disciples who saw him, talked with him, ate with him, amused and annoyed him, but of those millions since who have not seen and yet have believed—never will see until that fulfillment that we cannot imagine except under such misty ideas as the coming of wholeness and the end of the partial.

We never come to the end of learning the meaning of this, that to live by faith is to have God but not, or only very rarely indeed, in the warm comfort of the feelings. What authenticates his presence is not any temporary emotional excitement but the slow freeing of our love so that we are able to express more of our self lovingly and have less need to withdraw or resist. It is a long-term result; we shall have to wait a long time to be assured of it. For the time being, for now, faith is a cool affair; some would call it bleak, but one comes to like it so. Emotion is a tricky adjunct to religious experience; it easily makes fools of us unless it is the warmth of the mature and integrated person's response to life. Till we become that we had best cast a cold eye on our feelings. What we want is meaning in our life, the drawing of the scattered and squandered self into a unity, less self-concern, more response to the next person, to beauty, to pain, to the fun of life, to reality. It is indeed God that we want.

Chapter 13

THE COMING OF
THE HOLY SPIRIT

The Christian experience with which the life of the
church began cannot be discovered by looking back
into the past, however sophisticated the means we use for
the study of bygone times. But the life of the church has
always had certain essential features in the centuries in
which it has been recorded. There is no reason to think
that it was any different in the earliest period for which
evidence is either absent or very scanty, so that it is true to
say that it is possible to know now what the initial
Christian experience was then. The essential Christian
experience is the conviction of the presence of Christ in
spite of his death, the realization that the facts about Jesus
make it possible to make profound and happy sense of
existence, and consequently the readiness to see Jesus as
deserving most of the great words that tradition had hith-
erto reserved for God.

The only aspect of the first disciples' entry into this
experience that we cannot capture now is the tremendous
excitement of its impact on minds that had for several
weeks been swept by a great sea of despair and joy and

question. As their confidence grew, their renewed commitment to Jesus and joy in his presence demanded expression. There came to the Christian group an irresistible desire to share with the rest of the world its joy in this new way of living life and understanding its meaning. The coming of this desire was itself a further range of spiritual experience, and Pentecost was the culminating joy and vision in which the group virtually became the Christian church.

St. Luke's account of this is written in the intense language which deep experience of God uses throughout the Bible (Acts 2:1–13). It is a language of fact and symbol and echo of the past and anticipation of what is to come. The sound from heaven, the rushing mighty wind, the fire are familiar images for the presence of God in the Bible and indeed in the literature of many faiths. The tongues of fire, resting on each Christian, signify the divine presence as speech, God's speech, given to each believer to say whatever is his part of the total message and mission of the church. In the crowds of pilgrims, drawn from all over the Mediterranean world, filling the streets of Jerusalem, the writer sees the fulfillment of that mission, soon to begin from Jerusalem, in which ultimately all the nations of the world will hear the story of Jesus each in its own language. He sees too, in the incomprehension of the public and the accusation of drunkenness, a darker side of that coming history in the inevitable alienation of the believing community. The future will not be a tale of unmitigated triumph; in every generation the Christian church, in order to be true to its Lord, will find itself at odds with its world, to which it will indeed seem at times eccentric, at times quite ridiculous.

The tongues of fire image signifies the two ideas of inspiration and word, the presence within the church and the church's mission to the world. Once we have come into faith, even only just into it, along with the desire to live and love in the light of the unique Son of Man another desire grows—in some way to share this new light for living. The church has tried many ways of commending Christian faith and must continually try out new ways as it learns from its mistakes or as one generation needs a different mode of encounter with the gospel from the one its predecessor found meaningful. But authentic Christian faith is bound to increase our openness to the world and our interest in it, not to conquer it and annex it to the empire of ecclesiastical statistics but to love it in Christ and to be sensitive to all in it that directly or indirectly points to him.

The word that carries the Christian experience of God's presence must itself be the word of God. The account of Pentecost is sometimes read as suggesting a universal ecstatic language which anyone will understand whatever his native tongue. There is such a language, though it is not an ecstatic one. It is the language of faith and love and hope. Everyone in the world longs to be loved and trusted, desires to know what we can trust and what we can hope for, and can respond when faith and love and hope are presented to us.

Jesus had supreme command of this tongue that meets the needs of all men so deeply. It was noted that he spoke with authority and not as the official exponents of religion like priests, ministers, teachers who have to do so much of the official speaking for religion. Because they have to do so much officially they sometimes settle for merely expounding and exhorting; sometimes they grow too closely identified with their own hopes for the church and become anxious and defensive, trying too hard to persuade. The world is bored with information and resists exhortation, believing that no one has the right to exhort.

The peculiar authority of Jesus' presence and language is to be traced to the fact that he was not defending anything, not even God, least of all himself. He spoke the truth about life as he saw it, living in the affectionate way in which he chose to live. The world that heard him, like ours, wanted to know why so much has to be endured, wanted life to be more than a succession of signs that we are not as free as we want to be, but could not see that he knew the way into anything better—though here and there people heard him with an irresistible stirring of hope or dismay, not because they were religious but because there was life in what he said.

It was these few who had come under the spell of Jesus who were so much more successful with his ideas than he. They found themselves in possession of the tongue of fire, the word that carries the presence of God, when they reached the point of thorough conviction about Jesus and his place in life. Their sharing this conviction with the world meant the expansion of the church.

But the expansion of the church is not the only sign of the presence of the Spirit in the words and acts of convinced Christians. Fire is an intense word for God in the language of Christian experience. Sometimes it means pain, sometimes purification, sometimes love, because God's presence is found to be a kind of pain to the self-preoccupied, a purification to those whose lives move slowly between sin and forgiveness towards him, a flame of love to the blessed in paradise. In each individual Christian life and in the general life of the church God is found still to come as this pain and this purification and this love.

Today it seems that God is leading the church through considerable humiliation and self-questioning to a new understanding of his will. Jesus persuaded Nicodemus to think of God as unpredictable as the wind but never to doubt his power to work his will in any situation. This would work out just now in alertness and expectancy and detachment and perhaps particularly the endurance of uncertainty. It is easy to long for faith and not to notice that one is really wanting nothing much more than freedom from doubt. Doubt has always been one of the principal ingredients of faith ever since it was discovered that faith is like walking through strange country on a dark night. When the church is in the power of the Spirit it is in the hands of a reality that makes and breaks, uses and discards, lets die and resurrects. It could be the case sometimes, perhaps now, that if the one catholic and apostolic church is to be holy it will not be obviously successful.

The church believes it has been promised God's presence in the form of guidance into the truth. The truth that is meant is not every kind of truth—the truth of the physical sciences, for example—but the truth about God and his purpose in the world and what he wants done in particular situations.

God guides us principally through our reason because this, with our power to love, forms that characteristic of human being which represents the image of God. Our reason includes what is sometimes called our conscience. The conscience is not some unique faculty by which we come to wisdom. The conscience is simply the mind when it is making moral judgments, when it is estimating the right and wrong in a proposed course of action. The Christian approach to questions of right and wrong involves extensive self-examination, the attempt to understand one's motives, the awareness of the amount of self-interest there is in the decision one is on the point of making. The emphasis on inwardness and motive was a constant one in Jesus' teaching about behavior, and it inevitably makes decisions more difficult to reach. Our motives form the most intimate and confused background to our behavior. For this reason they are only partially open to us.

But it is in the whole life of the individual that God's guidance comes, not just in the operation of a part of the personality. Particularly the Christian believes that all that he does to cultivate his life of faith, through prayer and reading and exploring the image of Christ in the gospels, informs his mind and makes it sensitive to the influence of the Spirit so that he increasingly reacts to life in a Christian way.

Even so we must not expect always or even often to serve God in a perfect harmony of the self. Most of the time we only partially want God, the rest of us being a turmoil of fears and hates and wants that have little to do with him. However, the service of God is done with the will, not with the feelings. It is possible to fix the will in a God-ward direction, to want to serve him in the deepest part of the self, even though the rest of us is to all intents and purposes religiously dead. We cannot expect to move towards God all in one piece like a saint. The best we shall reach is this turning of the will to God again and again while the emotional side of us either pulls in some other direction or seems completely inert. This division of the self into two, a top half which is excitable and easily disturbed, and a deeper part that is more real, quieter, wiser and can be fixed on God though the upper part is a revolting mess—this idea has been much used by the saints, and ordinary Christians still find it helpful. St. Teresa believed that the most important events in God's dealings with us happen in this deeper self and may therefore not be obvious.

Sometimes the person seeking the guidance of God has to put up with the fact that it may be God's will, perhaps for reasons known only to him, that this trusting Christian should be in uncertainty. Often the sense of certainty comes as we approach the time when action is necessary. Before that point we simply have to wait in faith.

God's guidance is not an interruption of the normal flow of life, a special occasion. It is with us all the time because his presence is with us all the time. His present guidance is generally clear.

We can generally know now what he wants us to do now. We cannot always know now what he will want us to do in the future. If we are thinking out a problem and light does not come, it is right to regard that as present guidance. Having done all the thinking we fruitfully can about the matter, we have clearly to endure the obscurity of the situation, and we had better leave the perplexing issue and give ourselves to the immediate duty or pleasure that is in front of us. There is always something God wants us to do now. It must always be one thing. It must always be something that we can do.

We should not assume that, because we believe in the guidance of the Spirit and have prayed and thought about the problem, the decision we finally come to will be the most prudent we could have reached and must be successful. God is wisdom and truth. We perceive this wisdom and truth imperfectly. Our conscience may be ill-informed or immature. The decision to which our minds finally come may be the wrong one. We may not always know what is the will of God in the sense of that which he wants done in this particular situation, but it is always God's will that we do that which in an attitude of prayer and extensive thought and faith we believe to be the best course. And when we have done that we can say that we have done God's will. But we say it in faith and humility, already asking for forgiveness, because we know that somewhere in it all there will be failure on our part—and leaving the issue to that fatherly providence which eternally directs and redirects the movement of life, and can, without invading their freedom, make the mistaken insights of men serve his purpose as long as they love him and want his will to prevail.

Our prayer for the guidance of the Spirit does not expect that the situation will be changed into some form more in accordance with our wishes or our strength. It is a means of expressing our Christian outlook, providing words for our deepest intention, and can be seen as the Holy Spirit bringing to our remembrance the things of Christ. One of the "things of Christ" is the conviction that though life continually eludes calculation and manipulation there is always something for love to do. As we dwell on this we find ourselves defining the situation in new terms; some of our original wishes concerning it are seen to be quite irrelevant, and it becomes clear that there is in fact a way forward and a grace to be relied on.

In seeking the truth about how we should act in one situation after another we are faced with our limitations in knowledge and in time for the necessary thought. The Christian is concerned about national and international problems. His mind cannot rest in the view that no action is required from the average church member because he has not studied sufficiently the complexities of British trade unionism or Greek politics or the problem of race in South Africa. History is made through a glass darkly by people whose decisions are a mixture of insight and prejudice and guess. The view that action should be left to the well-informed relieves practically all of us of political and social responsibility.

It is part of humility to accept the limitations of the human condition. Most situations calling for decision are a mixture of right and wrong. It is rarely possible to find the whole truth—certainly of anything as complicated as a political event. This is not the sort of world in which it can be expected that any problem will be perfectly solved or any arrangement will work entirely satisfactorily. It is therefore a world in which humans cannot afford to indulge themselves in pride and self-confidence because these close the mind to the grace we so obviously need.

But it is also a world in which cruelty and greed and triviality thrive too easily and what is human and civilizing continually needs encouragement. We know we must responsibly inquire as far as we can, but we know too that we must act, and we shall most of the time have to act before we have it all clear. It is not the Christian view that people who so act are more likely to be right because they act in Christian faith. It is more a question of what being right really is. If God is working through the response of men to their circumstances, all the time leading us, if we are willing, into a deeper experience of faith and love, it will not in the end be a question of "Who was right?" but

"Who cared? Who sensed the essential obscurity and left room for compassion?" On this view nevertheless, as a character in one of Graham Greene's novels says, it is better to have blood on one's hands than water.

There are situations in which it seems there is nothing we can do now, but that cannot be true for a Christian. There is always God's will to be done. Even when the worst comes to the worst we shall inevitably do something. We can turn our back on it and attempt some way of not believing it, or we can hate life the more because such things happen in it, or we can set foot on some private path of slow self-destruction through despair, or we may be given grace to take it all, to open ourselves to the pain, feeling all that sensitive human nature will feel and lifting up to God the various decisions we must now make in a life so mutilated. But we shall be bound to do something. Every moment of every day is a moment in which we shall do God's will in faith—or do something else. It is part of the purpose of Christian prayer to enable us to come to terms with life so that whatever happens it will not come between us and God, and we shall still set ourselves to love him and man, glad of a life in which that good thing is possible.

Sometimes, when our own endurance is not at stake but someone else's, we may reluctantly conclude that there is nothing we can do. Our lives may be too closely involved in common experience and relationship. In marriage and family life, for instance, suffering can often only be relieved by the affection and insight of people who are not bound up in the same bundle of life. We may see no way of helping in the immense sufferings of war or natural disaster thousands of miles away from us. We may have to watch someone we love apparently disintegrating morally or drifting away from us into the bleak solitariness of neurosis. Yet in such situations there must be something God wants done by us.

We can pray. Our praying is the expression of our love for the people we so remember, and love must always be of use to God. Our praying is the expression of our faith in God regarding them, and faith involves us in enduring our own anxiety and lack of skill or ability to help, in trusting rather than throwing other people's pain in God's face. Life must always be deeply helped by faith and love. It may be that our separation from one another, our individuality, is only physical. Loving may be a form of living in which at some untraceable depth human beings are united and give and receive unknown good. We believe that this happens with special intensity throughout the great communion of the church on earth and in heaven. We do not understand the nature of this mutuality but we believe that it is God's will to bind us to himself and to each other and that in every true moment of faith and love far more is involved than we can see; indeed heaven and earth are involved, as the *Sanctus* in the Eucharist declares.

Praying is not merely the offering of words or silence to God, it is the offering of oneself to God. The offering of self, which takes the form of prayer for someone we cannot directly help because of distance or inability, will become the awareness of something close at hand to be undertaken. The love that can only express itself in action to benefit the particular person we love—and must be suspended in frustration if such action is not possible—is an extremely immature love with a considerable element of compulsive attachment in it.

As the life, death, and resurrection of Jesus are continually remembered and explored in the life of the church its members have a unique experience of God. It is a corporate experience of the Spirit and it makes the church a fellowship of the Spirit. There is of course fellowship of the Spirit in Judaism and Islam, to take just two examples. The church differs from these in that its fellowship is constituted by the fact that it knows God through Christ; the

Spirit that animates it proceeds from the Father and the Son.

At Pentecost the life of the fellowship began with tongues of fire. The fire which is God's presence must be communicated, must become the word of a message and a mission. This word is spoken by the whole life of the church, its sacramental life, its worship, its teaching, its diversified witness and suffering. Sometimes this word is clear and persuasive, sometimes it is obscure indeed. The world, too, seems to have periods in which the need for religious meaning is very near the surface of life and at other times to want, perhaps even need, other forms of meaning far more. But at all times the church's task is the same. The Virgin Mary is a figure of the church in Christian tradition. Her place in Christian devotion is certainly a continual reminder of the church's mission and the need to consider what form that mission should currently take. Just as in bearing Jesus she gave form to that with which she was inspired by the Holy Spirit, Christ himself, so the church is continually involved in giving expressive form to its inspiration, the knowledge of God through Christ it carries within its common life.

Many people think that if this is its high task the church should be a more impressive affair than it is, but they are not able to say how impressive a fellowship would have to be for them to believe God was in it. Much in the life of the church is certainly perplexing; in parts it is discreditable; everyone is disappointed with it. But people who stay in it long enough to appreciate its life in some depth still find their anxiety about sin and death loosening its hold, their self-preoccupation dispersing in a broader, richer response to life, and think it reasonable to call this the grace of our Lord Jesus Christ. There is also in the church today a sharp, unsatisfied longing for God, a desire for freshness in Christian utterance because most Christian preaching and teaching are just now so deficient in vitality and interest, and an intense, perturbed self-questioning. This also is the presence of God. It has been part of Christian experience of God from the beginning. St. Paul writes dramatically about this characteristic Christian distress as a condition in which we do not know what to think about God or say to him and can only groan and fumble to express ourselves in struggles and longings that seem to be part of a great universal travail. It was his view that God is particularly present and deeply working there.

Chapter 14

THE ASSUMPTION OF THE VIRGIN MARY

Eugene Ionesco wrote in his journal:

> Supposing we did not die. No one would hate anyone
> any more. No one would ever again be envious of any-
> one. We would love each other. We could go on indefi-
> nitely making a fresh start, and from time to time some-
> thing would be accomplished. At the hundredth or thou-
> sandth attempt, we would meet with success. The sheer
> number of the attempts would make this possible. We
> know that we haven't time to try our luck indefinitely.
> Hatred is the expression of our anguish, of our lack of
> time. Jealousy is the expression of our fear of being aban-
> doned, first in life, then in death.

The Christian stands with everyone thus perplexed by
mortality. Christians also feel that unless we can in some
sense see through death by faith, life is hardly worth it,
because the light we have to work by is so brief. We sometimes feel this so keenly that we are apt to exaggerate the

problem. People can and do find meaning in their lives, living it well and finding under some other name what we call communion with God, without needing to see death cut down to manageable size. They keep their bearings by reference to relative and local significances, even negotiating calamity, without the help of traditional religious interpretations, without needing them.

It is different for those who have come to see life in Christian terms. If we believe that the meaning of life is that we are here to learn with increasing sensitiveness and competence what faith and love are, we want to see a little further ahead. One earthly life is ludicrously short for such a task as learning faith and love. And we must think too, though it can only be by means of the language of myth and symbol, of the purpose of life *completed* in an ultimate fulfillment of knowing and loving. We cannot commit ourselves to a purpose that we suspect will never be realized.

It is not only that a life beyond death seems implied in the purpose for which we have been created. The learning of the kind of love and trust that so powerfully appeal to us in the life of Christ gives life such a pervading significance, to the minutest detail of experience, and opens the mind to so many new forms of satisfaction, that the Christian wants much more of this kind of life. He becomes convinced of its rightness; the proof is in the living, and he begins to sense a new desire welling up within him—to see face to face the one who he believes is never absent from his life, of whom he intermittently thinks he is aware. This desire becomes expectancy as he increasingly interprets his assurances of the presence of God as the long shadows cast by the coming blessedness of the great fulfillment.

They are inexpressibly long shadows. We cannot think of blessedness as a radiance on which the door of death immediately opens. Death cannot give us more than a new range of opportunity for learning and doing the love of

God, because we have so much yet to learn. It cannot give us paradise. But we believe that growth in knowledge and love of God will not come to nothing, it will culminate in the everlasting joy of the kingdom as the deep sea wave curls for the last time and falls on the sunlit shore.

That joy is not the reward of it all. It is the completion and fulfillment of a life which all the way through is infinitely worthwhile and so has no room for any reward other than itself infinitely developed and extended. People who pray in the Christian way find that the wants they wish to make the subject of prayer steadily reduce in number and become increasingly dominated by the one desire to know God's will throughout the whole range of one's experience and to have the grace to do it. But at the same time, with a quite inexplicable desire, they long for this fulfillment, to see God as he is, not glimpsed through some veil.

It was an Old Testament dream that certain saintly people (Elijah, Enoch) would either transcend the full experience of death or be the subjects of a mysterious acceleration of it and be carried straightway into the presence of God. This dream came alive in the imagination of the early church as they thought of the mother of Jesus after her death.

However many or few years of fellowship with the first-generation church remained to her after Pentecost, she would have had a place of deepening affection and awe in their minds. She may well have fulfilled the maternal role in terms of which the church has interpreted Jesus' dying words to the beloved disciple: "There is your mother." It is clear that the church found it increasingly difficult to exclude her from their praise of Christ because the more sure they became of the glory of God in the face of Jesus and the more deeply they understood what the glory of God must be, the more they saw her irradiated by it.

By some instinct of tradition their minds began to move along an ancient path. They began to think of her as delivered from the total onslaught on us that death is, untouched by the indignity of physical corruption, certainly needing no further discipline of love, and raised into the glory of God's presence.

These ideas carry the full significance of the mythical in that while they cannot be associated with historical evidence they channel a deep stream of hope and conviction about the nature of life as life is understood in the Christian community. They belong to that community's inner life of love and prayer, as Orthodoxy so rightly pleads, not to its public proclamation to the world. As people pray and explore the mystery of Christ in the life of the church their minds will be drawn to dwell on this first lover of Christ, totally given as a mother to preparing him to meet and serve his world and God, and they will find themselves wanting to use this representative image of her as having arrived, the first of us all to have arrived, the earnest of what it all comes to in Christ.

To see her fulfillment as a bodily assumption is to have a comprehensive sign of the dignity given by Christian faith to the whole person. It is a way of celebrating human nature in prayer and particularly illustrates the fact that the Christian attitude to the body has been more imaginative in the prayer of the church than in its moral theology.

The religious mind has found several ways of representing a life after death but it has usually found little room for the physical there. Christianity has not escaped this view of the body as the underprivileged partner of the mind and the soul, destined to be discarded, much of the time a nuisance. But the body has fought back marvelously, sometimes terribly with the ferocity of a slighted goddess in a Greek tragedy. God has not left it long without witnesses to its truth, and there have been voices of great distinction to plead for its honor. What Michelangelo, Blake, Freud, D. H. Lawrence, and others have said for it in their art and wisdom is now seen to be true at many points to the mind of Jesus and is in our day refreshing the mind of the church.

It is God's will that we love him and our neighbor with all that there is to us, with our whole being as a thinking, feeling, acting self, its deeper levels as well as its conscious superstructure. To say that it is the whole self that is destined to reach the joy of the ultimate kingdom is the other side of the coin, another form of the conviction that it is God's will that we love him with the whole self now.

The Christian meditating the Assumption is affirming this faith and has its twin aspects in mind as he asks the Blessed Virgin Mary to pray for us now and at the hour of our death. God's will does not change. Because he is eternal it is no different now from what it will be then. He has ordained that human fulfillment is in loving just as much when this life is taken from us and another given us as now. It is by so doing his will with all that we are that we shall at length reach the glory that is hers.

That glory is imagined by the Christian mind as the fulfillment of all human potentiality, not as the refinement and satisfaction of some supposedly superior part of us. Nothing of value in our life is to be considered expendable or destined to disappear. "We do not want to have the old body stripped off. Rather our desire is to have the new body put on over it, so that our mortal part may be absorbed into life immortal. God himself has shaped us for this very end" (2 Cor. 5:4 NEB). That is St. Paul's attempt to say in prose what the mystery of the Assumption says in prayer. Human nature, made by God and pronounced good by him, is good forever, and accordingly it will reach its fulfillment by a process of transformation and elevation, not by the abandonment of one constituent at one stage and the sacrifice of another at another.

The meaning of the Assumption does not concern only human being. The human body belongs to the vast world of physical nature and cannot be understood in separation from it. And this also is part of the goodness of things. But in his ignorance and his greed man has violated and mis-used nature so that his belonging to nature is now a source of suffering as well as good for him. There is a further wrongness about the natural world that is a great mystery and trouble to us; the animal world seems such a complex of ruthless self-assertion, everything living by the destruc-tion of something else and eventually dying that some-thing else may live. We find it difficult to contemplate this with an easy mind. In some examples and forms it is absolutely revolting.

We are not the first to feel this. There is an Old Testament dream of a time when the ancient animal enmities will cease and man himself will not have the guilt of being against them, nor have to take their lives day after day.

> Then the wolf shall live with the sheep,
>   and the leopard lie down with the kid;
> the calf and the young lion shall grow up together,
>   and a little child shall lead them;
> the cow and the bear shall be friends,
>   and their young shall lie down together.
> The lion shall eat straw like cattle;
>   the infant shall play over the hole of the cobra,
>   and the young child dance over the viper's nest.
> They shall not hurt or destroy in all my holy mountain.
>   (Isaiah 11:6–9)

People who see human life as a learning of love are bound to share this perplexity about the world of nature and this dream of an ultimate reconciliation there. Otherwise their hopes for their own deliverance and sur-vival must stand condemned for discreditable self-con-cern. Certainly the Bible does not encourage such ego-tism. Its message is not that there is some future state awaiting human beings who accordingly can take heart to carry on; it is that ultimately God will achieve his purpose and be all in all. With this hope in mind St. Paul states his

belief that the whole creation, at present subject to disso-
lution and death (a condition he calls vanity or futility),
will eventually be liberated into a freedom in which each
created thing can fulfill the potentialities of its being
without having to challenge the fulfillment of another.

This is such an infinitely superior way of thinking to
that which states the problem simply in terms of human
survival or resurrection that one wonders why the church
has not made more of it. The kind of religion that proposes the ultimate in terms of "that will be glory for me" is
psychologically infantile and morally disgusting. It is a
religion of self-regard not of love. The Christian faith
desires to outline a fulfillment of life that is consistent
with a religion of love. Love cannot be confined to the
realm of personal relationships and personal needs. It
includes the artist's and the scientist's respect and wonder
at the grain and structure of the material world, the realization that the world of nature is infinitely knowable and
may well be discovered to have other significances for its
Creator than to be merely the stage upon which the drama
of God and man takes place, and the refusal to entertain
any idea of the fulfillment of life that does not include all
mankind and the whole created universe. What we long
for is the transformation of nature into a clear manifesta-
tion of the love of God till all is glory and grace, not an
escape from it or an abandonment of it at some point at
which we imagine it has served its purpose as an adjunct
of human life.

Religious faith does not have the words, nor the duty,
to explain how this may be. It has its symbols and myths
and poetic images to carry the desire of the mind as it
prays with the church. Such explication of this desire as is
possible will be done by philosophers and scientists in
terms of their own world of discourse as they are led by the
Spirit.

The mystery of the Assumption, like all Christian
imagery of eternity, is not to be understood merely or pri-

marily chronologically, as referring to a life infinitely beyond this life, but existentially, as involving us in responsibilities and decisions now and providing a confidence and tranquility in which to fulfill responsibilities and make decisions.

The mind that is continually refreshed with the celebration of nature and human nature will be concerned about all that abuses the one and degrades the other. It will develop a new sensitiveness to waste and ugliness and pollution and economic injustice and will want to act with such forces as are set to diminish them. That part of the redemption of matter which God wills to do *in* man and *with* man he will not do *for* man. The Christian believes in an ultimate transformation of the whole creation in a fulfillment in which God will be all in all. But an essential part of that transformation is the learning of faith and love by human beings in this life and in whatever further ranges of existence God provides for them. Yet the prevailing tone of Christian faith is not uncertain but optimistic. The characteristic Christian attitude is sensitiveness to the decidedly untransformed condition of this world and certainty that "all shall be well and all manner of things shall be well." Such confidence makes no sense at all as an isolated comment on the way things may be expected to go, but for those who live life by faith in Christ and within the fellowship and prayer of the Christian community, it makes the sort of sense that enables them to work without limit since they believe that in the Lord their labor cannot be in vain, to enjoy without sadness since there shall never be one lost good, and to suffer without despair because by suffering in faith and love the transformation of their evil into good has already begun.

It is true that skeptics and humanists work with persistence, love the goodness and beauty of life, suffer creatively and without resentment. They differ from the Christian in their understanding of the way life goes. They love knowing that everything dies, nothing is stronger than death, all comes to death, and there is no long view to take when you see someone spoiling your work or some unearned suffering draining a life of all possibility of fulfillment in this world. The Christian loves in a mental atmosphere of faith and hope. Faith and hope hold love up when it is badly wounded, help it to recover, encourage it to try loving again even when it has been betrayed. This kind of outlook is something of a necessity for our times. We have had traumatic experiences of how evil man can be and are perhaps getting used to what is monstrous. We give an odd prestige to the pathological and the disgraceful and seem to want to play in this dark element. It is the wrong path for civilization. The Christian church has a huge ministry of encouragement to perform and must join its special form of hope and joy to other forms, to strengthen in the world all that is for human beings and their future.

> If this life be not a real fight, in which something is eternally gained for the universe by success, it is no better than a game of private theatricals from which one may withdraw at will. But it feels like a real fight—as if there were something really wild in the universe which we, with all our idealities and faithfulnesses, are needed to redeem; and first of all to redeem our own hearts from atheisms and fears. For such a half-wild, half-saved universe our nature is adapted.[12]

Chapter 15

THE QUEEN
OF HEAVEN

When Christians pray they do so as part of a religious community in which they have been given membership. This community, the church, is the place where the presence of God in Christ is thankfully known and allowed to have its own way as much as the love and trust of believers dare to let it. No other community in the world exists for this purpose. It is from this group that the believer has learned to pray, to use its language and its spiritual tradition; and it is within this group that he discovers more of what it means to know the presence of Christ.

The Christian religion is very much a community affair while being at the same time intensely personal. Being a religion of love it must indeed see all isolation, whether of misunderstanding or guilt or resentment, as part of the wrongness of life. Accordingly, its view of the fulfillment of life is in community terms, as an ultimate fellowship of loving in which all men and things are loved in the love of God, not the love that excludes because it is the intense predilection of one person for another, of one person for some part of reality, but the loving that is simply the way all will live and have their being.

The community of faith, in which Christians are learning to discern and love the presence of God and living in hope of this ultimate fulfillment, is infinitely vast, stretching through time as well as space. Christians who have died still belong to the one Christian family and are believed to be still occupied in the great purpose of learning faith and love within it. They loved us, we loved them, when they were here. In Christ we know that all that loving can still go on, that there is nothing to stop this mutual grace and joy.

This is an integral part of the Christian way of living, the Christian joy in the continuity of life. None of us can be saved by his own efforts; none of us can be saved alone. We cannot have God without the whole company of heaven and the whole unsatisfactory company of the church on earth. All fastidious attempts to go it alone cut us off from grace because they are refusals to abide in Christ. The only way in which we can come to our fulfillment is together, by praying for the fulfillment of all and with the help of the prayers of all. God wills us to learn love in loving others and receiving love from others. He has given the church the Holy Spirit, shed it abroad throughout the whole body, to make this loving possible. The Spirit is the spirit of love. God does not change his will for those who have died, nor does he withdraw the Spirit from them. They have it still, to use in loving. So we continue to love them and pray for them, and we believe they love us and pray for us.

This sense of belonging together in Christ so that any ground lost by anyone affects the rest and any grace received involves the rest is made very clear in the form of confession in the revised Roman Mass in which priest and people say together:

I confess to almighty God, and to you, my brothers and sisters, that I have sinned through my own fault in my thoughts and in my words, in what I have done, and in what I have failed to do; and I ask blessed Mary, ever virgin, all the angels and saints, and you, my brothers and sisters, to pray for me to the Lord our God.

Christians have particularly sought the prayers of those of the departed whose love and faith have deeply excited the admiration and affection of the church. It is natural for Christians in their private praying to ask for the prayers of anyone whom they particularly love and reverence; it is equally natural for the church in its public prayer to ask for the prayers of those whom it particularly loves and honors, the saints, in whom it believes God's will for the church is exceptionally clear.

As the church has remembered the saints it has seen a special glory surrounding those who knew Jesus in his earthly life. But even that glory is a pale thing in comparison with that radiance which it has come to see around the mother of Jesus. She was the one who made his human presence possible, planted his young mind with the memories that were the seed of all his spontaneity and courage, taught him what loving is. The mysterious and holy importance of her being suggested a further role for her in the life of the church.

As the years go on and the church's memory becomes long, its experience of the communion of saints, of the continual giving and receiving of love throughout the whole body, becomes so full of meaning that the mind cannot comprehend it. There is the need for some form and instance of it all to stand clear and lovable in the mind and be the particular through which the whole is represented. Nothing could be more natural than that Christians should find this in the Blessed Virgin Mary, their most loved sister in Christ, the first Christ-lover and model of the Christ-centered life, the sign of the call and destiny of the church. Representing all, she becomes the Queen of Saints whose prayers all lovers of Christ need and want, to help them love him more and serve him better.

In the rosary the mother of Jesus is not asked for anything other than her prayers. In the public worship of the church she and the saints are normally only asked for their prayers. The private prayer of the Christian is rightly freer, and in this freedom, under influences of temperament or personal need or misunderstanding of the truth as it is in Christ, it may take forms which may be difficult to justify. But Christian praying is learned primarily not in isolation but within a tradition, in communion with the whole church in the liturgy. By continually taking his personal praying into the common prayer of the church the believer exposes it to enlargements and purifications that save it from eccentricity and immaturity.

The church understands the prayers of the saints to be an infinite multiplicity of one and the same request—that we may all love God and do his will in Christ and that with the whole creation we may come to his heavenly kingdom. Nothing is worth praying for beside this. The saints, whose lives are so much more given to God than ours, see this with a deeper certainty than we do, but we also know that God wills to give us grace to grow in faith and love until that which is perfect is come, and that this is the sum and substance of all good. Anyone who wants anything more than this or other than this is living another life altogether. It may, of course, be magnificent, but it is not the life of Christian faith.

But a Christian prayer for others is not a mere voicing of a request to God to help the person who is just now in the foreground of our love, as though we do the asking and God does the helping. It is to detach our affection from our predilections and anxieties concerning this person and to love him within our thankfulness that God is what he is and acts as he does, and then to offer ourselves to God for the carrying out of any part of his purpose for this loved individual that he may lay upon us. Accordingly, to pray for others always involves the person who prays in some action for God that will carry part of God's answer.

In what way the Blessed Virgin Mary and the saints and the departed who pray for us carry their due part of God's aid to us we cannot know. What we can be sure about is that they do so serve God and us, because this is what prayer is and because God wills to bless all through all. We can be sure, too, that their unseen service to us is entirely to help us trust and love God and life more.

It is not only as a sign of the church and the representative figure of its love of Christ that the mother of Jesus holds the Christian mind. Many other Christian associations find their point of concentration in her. The value of these associations as expressing Christian faith and love must vary from person to person, perhaps being closely related to temperamental characteristics. It may well ebb and flow with changes in psychological need in the individual's life.

That she is the mother of the Son of God is naturally the starting point of all the Christian love and amazement that have gathered round her. She stands too near to so much glory for faith to be content with seeing her just as any other creature.

But towards this glorified mother there has poured a great flood of emotion from the conscious and unconscious mind throughout the Christian centuries. It seems that at the basis of all developed religions there is one form or another of a sky divinity who is male and an earth divinity who is female. At one time or another the Blessed Virgin Mary has absorbed the attributes of the primordial earth goddess who had a threefold relationship to Zeus as mother, bride, and daughter.

It is not possible, nor desirable, to prevent religious experience stirring the deepest levels of the mind and activating our most ancient and involuntary race memories.

The most expressive Christian liturgy and art has always drawn some of its power from such depths. But we shall want what we say about the most holy mother of our Savior to have other justification than that interesting connections are traceable between it and the ancient paganisms that we have outgrown.

The Virgin Mary's motherhood is a particular aspect of her being that will always have meaning for some Christians and perplexity for others. In *The Spirit of Catholicism* Karl Adam writes, for example, "She is mother not of the Redeemer alone, but also of the redeemed; and so she is the mother of the faithful. The Catholic acknowledges in heaven not only a Father, but also a mother." But not all Christians who love the mother of Jesus are going to find such language expresses their mind. Indeed this way of thinking about Mary, as *our* mother, did not become common in the Christian world until about the tenth century, and only in the west.

Similarly, many Christians must be mystified by signs in Marian devotion of the desire to make her in some sense the lay figure for a romantic dream about the supposedly saving power of "the eternal feminine" (given schmaltzy expression in the final chorus of Goethe's *Faust*) or the bearer of feminine and maternal features of love which are said to be lacking in the orthodox Christian idea of God the Father's love.

There is no such lack in God's love. It is Christian belief that God is entirely love, and his love has been revealed in Jesus. It is for faith to discover the multitudinous forms of this love as it is expressed elsewhere in a thousand places—in the simpler perfection of the subhuman care of an animal for its young as well as in personality, in the love of friends, lovers, parents, in an artist's self-giving to his art, in a researcher's absorption in his subject, in all forms of human helping things to come right, in happiness, in difficulty, and eventually even in the pain of life—sufficiently, at any rate, to support the view that even if man makes his bed in hell God is there.

Among these presences of love Christians see with an infinite reverence and joy the Virgin Mary's love of God and of her mysterious son. Forever she is part of the church's praise of God for what he has done in Christ. But when we think of her as a sign in heaven it is not as a sign of some feminine love thought to be insufficiently clear in the love of the Blessed Trinity. God is the plenitude of love, a love that infinitely transcends the polarities of male and female, reason and emotion, joy and sorrow. For this reason he is present and worthy to be praised at all times and in all places.

It will always be the case that some forms of God's presence will have more meaning for us than others. We may be drawn to them by reasons of temperament, or at a particular stage of our spiritual growth, or in some personal crisis in which a particular aspect of God's revelation in Christ (perhaps Mary's motherhood) may hold in a single image a variety of spiritual wanting, hoping, and praising. The situation may then change and we are upheld and blessed by the consideration of other forms of God's infinite love. Every Christian must train himself to be glad that a form of prayer that may be no longer congenial to him is exactly right for someone else and that he himself must look for other helps now.

Since the Christian church sees in the Mother of God the supreme human figure of humble faith and love, and brings her image into so much of its prayer and praise, it will want to examine the providence that has resulted in so much meaning being centered in a woman.

God, the Holy Spirit, has led the church to need and love a woman's presence in its praying for many reasons, but one of them may be to prepare the mind of the church for its task of understanding the world of the feminine.

This task is now before the church as it is before the world. It is clear that for centuries we have taken for granted traditional ideas about the distinction between male and female and their different roles in life. All these assumptions are now disintegrating under the scrutiny of various intellectual disciplines.

Conventional stereotyping of male and female nature is being further challenged by rapid contemporary change in personal relationships, in family life, and the world of daily work. At the same time our generation finds heterosexual love a judgment, an exposure of its ignorance and emotional ineptitude and aggression, as well as the age-long channel of its desire to give, to make happy, to know joy. Its failure to understand the things that belong to love works out in an angry and irreverent taking sex to pieces which, as in all neurotic reactions, betrays obliquely the genuine desire to know the truth about love.

No profound and sensitive grasp of the truth about men and women is possible if it is done by men alone. Neither men nor women can understand the truth of their being alone. They will do this together, as each learns how the other sees and feels life, and as they discover what God has given to each to know about love that the other does not know, will never know except as they imaginatively and lovingly enter into each other's being.

The church that sees a woman of our race crowned with such a glory of meaning sees her also as a sign in heaven of God's call to our generation to this journey of discovery, to find and exalt the values which he wills the sexual realm to bear in human life.

The mother of Jesus is also a sign of Christianity's spiritual past from which it can never be free and will never want to be free, which nevertheless involves it in characteristic obligations and perplexities. The Annunciation that heralded the supreme revelation of God's love for man was made to a Jewish woman. The exaltation of the Blessed Virgin Mary is of one who belongs to that religion and people which form our root, our victim, and our shame. Positively, she is God's call to the church humbly and self-critically to consider its relations with Judaism and ask if it is not now time that these two great and related streams of spiritual life flowed more closely together. Negatively, she is a sign, perhaps especially in our grim age, of the enormity of the slightest suggestion of anti-Semitism in the Christian mind.

One title given to the mother of Jesus which must perplex many Christians is that of "Ever-Virgin." The truth hidden in this description can only be understood as part of the Christian praise of Christ that the fulfillment and completion of God's purpose has already begun in him. It does not refer to an event in the dimension of recorded time, accessible to human curiosity. Questions of historicity are as irrelevant to it as are the facts of Danish history to the significance of Shakespeare's *Hamlet*. The title "Ever-Virgin" draws on ancient forms of expression in man's long struggle to say what the divine must be and indicates thoughts for which we would use other terms, though they might well be no more effective. It means that, her Son being who he is, we see her as one called into a single, exclusive, unrepeatable part of the service of God, as being wholly involved in this spiritually and physically, hearing the word of God and keeping it with all her heart and soul and strength.

Its meaning extends in the thought of an emptiness of self that waits for God alone to fill it, a faith that endures losses and unmet longings and ungranted prayers, without running to compensations and distractions to fill the void, because it believes that God will give himself and his meaning in his own time. The Christian mind in meditation finds the Virgin Mary meaning this absolute openness to God and aspires to it, wants to breathe its free yet dedicated atmosphere.

And most deeply, as the ultimate fulfillment of God's purpose begins in Jesus, there is a sense in which it also begins in Mary, so that she is a sign of the first light of that kingdom of heaven where Jesus said there is neither marrying nor giving in marriage but only the fullness of love that transcends all the limitations and predilections of temporal sexuality.

All that the church says of her in its own language of prayer and the worship of God is to express and rejoice in its understanding of what God has done for us all in Christ. It does this by giving dramatic symbolic form to some implications of God's presence in Jesus that involve us in this grateful love and veneration of his mother. She is to faith a sign of many meanings that can be discerned with unique vividness through her image, but she is the sign of what the church thinks of Christ.

ENDNOTES

1. James Hillman, *Insearch* (Hodder and Stoughton, 1967), 99.
2. T. S. Eliot, *The Elder Statesman* (Faber and Faber, 1959), 71–2.
3. J. Goldbrunner, *Holiness is Wholeness* (Burns and Oates, 1955), 28.
4. D. E. Jenkins, *Jesus and God* (Faith Press, 1965), 80.
5. Max Thurian, *Mary, Mother of the Lord*, tr. N. Cryer (Faith Press, 1963), 107.
6. J. Jeremias, *The Prayers of Jesus* (SCM Press, 1967), 105.
7. Simone Weil, *Waiting on God* (Routledge and Kegan Paul, 1952), 38.
8. Henri de Lubac, *Paradoxes* (Editions du Seuil, 1959), 161.
9. Simone Weil, *Gravity and Grace* (Routledge and Kegan Paul, 1952), 67.
10. Dorothea Krook, *The Ordeal of Consciousness in Henry James* (Cambridge University Press, 1967), 335.
11. Tony Tanner, *Henry James* (Macmillan, 1968), 273.
12. William James, *The Will to Believe* (Dover Publications, 1956), 61.

www.ingramcontent.com/pod-product-compliance
Lightning Source LLC
Jackson TN
JSHW020020141224
75386JS00025B/618